Woman of Valor:
Conquering Toxic People God's Way

Karen Pless Gaines

All rights reserved. No part of this book may be produced in any form or by any electronic or mechanical means including information storage and retrieval systems—except in the case of brief quotations embodied in critical articles or reviews—without permission in writing to the publisher, Karen Pless Gaines

The characters and events portrayed in this book are fictional, meaning no real name are used except with permission. Any similarity to real persons, living or dead, is purely coincidental and not intended by the author.

The information used to write this book was public knowledge and is cited in the back of the book. For privacy reasons, real names have not been used in the making of this book.

Published by Karen Pless Gaines Toccoa Georgia,
karenplessgaines@outlook.com
Copyright © 2025 Karen Pless Gaines
All rights reserved.
ISBN: 979-8-9879003-3-8

DEDICATION

This book is dedicated to every woman who has endured the pain of toxic relationships, to those who have felt lost and broken, and to those who have bravely fought for their healing and wholeness. May these pages offer you solace, hope, and the strength to rise above adversity, knowing that you are deeply loved, profoundly valued, and incredibly strong in the eyes of God. This is a testament to the unwavering power of faith, the human spirit's resilience, and our God's transformative love. It is dedicated to the women who have inspired me through their journeys of healing, courage, and unwavering faith. Although shared anonymously, their stories are woven throughout these pages, serving as beacons of hope for others traveling a similar path. This is a dedication to the quiet strength found in Christ, a testament to the healing power of His love, and a celebration of the indomitable spirit of women everywhere who choose to rise above. It's a tribute to the women who have shown me the depth of their faith and courage in the face of seemingly insurmountable obstacles, reminding me that God's love is always enough and that restoration is always possible. This book is for you.

CONTENTS

	Dedication	i
0	Introduction	1
1	Understanding Toxic Relationships and Their Impact	3
2	Establishing Healthy Boundaries	15
3	Healing From Past Trauma	33
4	Building Healthy Relationships	58
5	Discovering God's Purpose for Your Life	80
6	Moving Forward with Hope and Confidence	103
7	Real Life Stories	123
**	Expanded Learning and Group Study Question	136
*	Appendix/Glossary	143
*	Acknowledgements	149
*	About the Author	151

PREFACE

As a Christian life coach and pastor with experience counseling women who have survived toxic relationships and, based on my own experience, escaping and recovering from abusive relationships, I have witnessed firsthand the profound pain and devastation that such experiences can inflict. I've also been privileged to witness the remarkable journey of healing and restoration as these courageous women turned to their faith to find strength, hope, and liberation. This book is born from those encounters, from countless hours spent listening, praying, and offering guidance based on biblical principles and practical strategies. It is my hope that "Woman of Valor: Conquering Toxic People God's Way" will serve as a compassionate guide, offering a safe space for healing and empowerment. Within these pages, you will find a blend of biblical insights, practical advice, and real-life stories that demonstrate the possibility of breaking free from abusive patterns, rebuilding your life on a foundation of faith, and discovering the incredible woman God created you to be. This is not just a self-help book; it is a journey of faith, a testament to God's restorative power, and an invitation to embrace the beautiful, empowered future that awaits you. I pray that this book will provide you with the tools, the comfort, and the spiritual strength needed to embark on this transformative journey, allowing God's love to heal, renew, and empower you. Remember that your healing is possible, and God's grace is always sufficient.

INTRODUCTION

Are you feeling trapped in a cycle of toxic relationships? Do you yearn for freedom from emotional manipulation, control, or abuse? If so, you are not alone. Many women experience the pain of unhealthy relationships, leaving them feeling lost, broken, and unworthy. But I want you to know that there is hope, healing, and restoration available. "Woman of Valor: Conquering Toxic People God's Way" is designed to be your compassionate guide on this transformative journey. This book isn't about assigning blame or dwelling on the past; instead, it's about empowering you to break free from unhealthy patterns, rediscover your worth in Christ, and build a future filled with healthy, God-honoring relationships. We will explore biblical principles that offer guidance and hope, offering practical strategies and actionable steps to help you navigate the challenges you face. Through personal stories (shared with anonymity and respect for confidentiality), you'll find encouragement and relatable experiences that affirm your journey. We will delve into the importance of establishing healthy boundaries, healing from past trauma, and forgiving yourself and others. Most importantly, we will uncover the incredible strength and value you possess as a daughter of the King, reminding you of your inherent worth and God's unwavering love. Prepare to embark on a journey of self-discovery, empowerment, and spiritual growth as we explore God's plan for your life—a life filled with joy, peace, and healthy relationships. Take a deep breath, and let's begin.

In the famous words of Lao Tzu:

A journey of a thousand miles begins with a single step.

Let's take that step…

**On page 136 you will find a study section for expanded learning or group study.

CHAPTER 1
Understanding Toxic Relationships and Their Impact

Understanding the insidious nature of toxic relationships is the first crucial step toward healing and building a life rooted in God's love and grace. Many women find themselves trapped in cycles of emotional pain, often struggling to identify the very dynamics that are slowly eroding their well-being. This isn't about blaming or judging; it's about gaining clarity and equipping ourselves with the knowledge to break free. The Bible consistently emphasizes the importance of healthy relationships, built on mutual respect, love, and support – a stark contrast to the manipulative and controlling environments characteristic of toxicity.

Let's begin by defining what constitutes a toxic relationship. It's not simply about disagreements or conflict; healthy relationships inevitably experience friction. Healthy conflict involves honest communication, a willingness to compromise, and a mutual desire to resolve issues constructively. However, toxic relationships are characterized by a pattern of manipulative behavior designed to control, undermine, and ultimately diminish the other person. This control can manifest in various ways, often subtly, making it difficult to identify.

One common tactic is gaslighting, a form of psychological manipulation where the abuser distorts reality to make the victim question their own sanity. For example, a husband might deny making a hurtful comment, even when the wife has witnesses. He might then suggest that she's overly sensitive or imagining things, leaving her confused and doubting her own perception of events. This constant questioning of reality can lead to significant emotional distress and self-doubt.

Another key indicator is control. This isn't always overt; it can be subtle and insidious. A controlling partner might dictate what their spouse wears, who they spend time with, or even what they eat. They might monitor their phone calls, emails, or social media activity, justifying this behavior under the guise of "concern" or "love." However, the underlying motive is control, aimed at restricting the victim's autonomy and independence. This control can extend to finances, limiting access to money or demanding complete financial transparency without reciprocation.

Emotional manipulation is another hallmark of toxic relationships. The abuser might use guilt trips, silent treatments, or threats to manipulate their partner's emotions and behavior. They might exploit the victim's vulnerabilities, playing on their fears or insecurities to get what they want. For instance, a mother might constantly criticize her daughter, focusing on her shortcomings, creating a sense of inadequacy and dependence. This constant barrage of negative criticism erodes the daughter's self-esteem and keeps her bound to her mother's manipulative control.

Verbal abuse is often overlooked but can be incredibly damaging. It encompasses a wide range of behaviors, including insults, name-calling, constant criticism, and threats. The abuser might use sarcasm and belittling remarks to undermine the victim's self-worth. This constant stream of negativity creates a hostile environment that damages the victim's emotional well-being. It's important to remember that even seemingly "small" instances of verbal abuse accumulate over time, leading to a significant impact on mental health. The seemingly minor cutting remarks – the constant put-downs, undermining of achievements, or sarcastic comments – chip away at self-worth gradually, just like water erodes stone.

Consider the example of a friendship where one friend constantly cancels plans, criticizes the other's choices, and only contacts the other when she needs something. While this might seem like just a friendship with flaws, it actually showcases classic toxic patterns. The lack of reciprocity, the constant negativity, and the self-serving behavior are all signs of a one-sided and ultimately damaging relationship. The consistent negativity can subtly wear down the other friend, leading to feelings of worthlessness or anxiety even outside of their interaction.

Another scenario could involve a family relationship in which one sibling consistently undermines the others' achievements, spreading gossip and trying to sabotage their efforts. Constant negativity, competition, and attempts at control are hallmarks of a toxic dynamic. This kind of toxicity within a family can be especially damaging, as it impacts one's sense of belonging and security. The family setting, typically intended as a source of love and support, becomes a source of anxiety and emotional stress.

Recognizing these patterns is crucial. The Bible speaks frequently about the importance of community and healthy relationships, but it doesn't endorse relationships that actively harm and diminish individuals. Proverbs 17:17 states, "A friend loves at all times, and a brother is born for adversity." This verse highlights the consistent, unwavering support characteristic of healthy relationships, a stark contrast to the conditional and manipulative nature of toxic ones.

These examples illustrate how toxic relationships can subtly erode a person's sense of self-worth and spiritual well-being. They highlight the importance of recognizing these subtle patterns to protect yourself and your spiritual growth. Understanding that such manipulation is not a reflection of your worth, but rather a symptom of the abuser's own internal struggles, is key to breaking free. This understanding offers a perspective of compassion, recognizing the pain the abuser might be experiencing, while not excusing their harmful behaviors.

Remember, recognizing the signs of toxicity is not about judging others; it's about protecting yourself. God calls us to love and forgive, but that doesn't mean we must endure abusive or manipulative relationships. He empowers us to set boundaries, to seek support, and to build a life filled with healthy, nurturing connections. The journey toward healing is often challenging, but with God's grace and guidance, it's a journey you can embrace with confidence and hope. This initial understanding is the foundation upon which we will build a stronger, healthier, and more fulfilling life, reflecting the love and grace of our Heavenly Father. The following sections will provide specific tools and strategies to help you navigate these challenges and emerge stronger in your faith.

The insidious nature of toxic relationships extends far beyond the immediate emotional pain; they inflict a deep spiritual and emotional toll that can leave lasting scars. While the outward manifestations might be obvious – the constant criticism, the manipulative control, the emotional manipulation – the deeper wounds often remain hidden, festering beneath the surface. Understanding this deeper impact is crucial for embarking on a path of healing and restoration.

One of the most significant consequences of toxicity is the erosion of self-esteem and confidence. Constant negativity, belittling remarks, and the constant undermining of one's achievements create a sense of inadequacy and self-doubt. The victim begins to question their own judgment, their abilities, and even their worth as a person. This relentless assault on self-worth can lead to depression, anxiety, and a profound sense of isolation. The individual may start to believe the lies whispered by the abuser, internalizing the negativity and accepting it as truth. This is a direct attack on the image of God within them, a distortion of the inherent worth and dignity each individual possesses as a child of God.

The spiritual consequences are equally profound. A toxic relationship can severely damage one's relationship with God. The constant stress, anxiety, and emotional turmoil can make it difficult to pray, read Scripture, or engage in spiritual practices. The victim may feel disconnected from God, experiencing a spiritual dryness or emptiness. This spiritual disconnect can lead to feelings of guilt and shame, further compounding the emotional distress. The individual might question God's love and protection, wondering why He allows such suffering. This questioning isn't a sign of weakness but a natural response to profound pain. It's important to remember that God's love remains steadfast, even in the midst of suffering. His grace is sufficient, and His power is made perfect in weakness (2 Corinthians 12:9).

The impact on mental health can be devastating. Prolonged exposure to toxic relationships can lead to various mental health conditions, including depression, anxiety, post-traumatic stress disorder (PTSD), and even suicidal ideation. Constant emotional abuse can leave deep psychological scars, affecting one's ability to form healthy relationships in the future. The victim might struggle with trust issues, fearing intimacy and closeness. This fear can manifest as emotional withdrawal or an inability to form genuine connections. It's crucial to seek professional help in such instances; a therapist can provide the necessary support and guidance to navigate these complex mental health challenges.

The Bible offers a powerful message of hope and restoration in the midst of such pain. Psalm 147:3 assures us, "He heals the brokenhearted and binds up their wounds." This verse speaks directly to the spiritual and emotional damage caused by toxic relationships. God is a healer, and His power extends to mend the deepest wounds of the heart and soul. He does not merely offer a temporary bandage; His healing is complete and transformative.

Isaiah 61:1-3 provides a profound promise of restoration: "The Spirit of the Sovereign Lord is on me, because the Lord has anointed me to proclaim good news to the poor. He has sent me to bind up the brokenhearted, to proclaim freedom for the captives and release from darkness, to comfort all who mourn, and to provide for those who grieve in Zion—to bestow on them a crown of beauty instead of ashes, the oil of joy instead of mourning, and a garment of praise instead of a spirit of despair. They will be called oaks of righteousness, a planting of the Lord for the display of his splendor." This passage speaks directly to the experience of those who have suffered the pain of toxic relationships. It promises freedom, healing, comfort, and a restoration of joy and beauty.

Self-Care is Vital—Not Selfish

The process of spiritual renewal after exposure to toxicity involves several key steps. First, it's crucial to acknowledge the pain and the impact it has had. Suppressing or denying the hurt only prolongs the healing process. Confessing the pain to God, a trusted friend, or a therapist allows for a release of pent-up emotions and opens the door to healing.

Next, forgiveness is essential, both for the abuser and for oneself. Forgiving the abuser does not mean condoning their actions; it means releasing the bitterness and resentment that binds us to the past. Forgiving oneself is equally important, releasing the self-blame and self-doubt that often accompany the experience of abuse. This is a crucial step in breaking free from the cycle of pain. Remember, God's love is unconditional and His forgiveness is limitless.

Seeking support is vital in the healing process. This might involve joining a support group, connecting with a trusted friend or mentor, or engaging in professional therapy. Sharing one's experiences with others who understand can provide validation, encouragement, and hope. It's important to find a community that offers compassion, understanding, and support without judgment.

Finally, it's essential to focus on self-care and spiritual growth. This might involve engaging in activities that bring joy and peace, such as spending time in nature, listening to uplifting music, or pursuing creative hobbies. Prioritizing prayer, Bible study, and other spiritual disciplines is vital in nurturing a stronger relationship with God and fostering inner peace. The healing process is a journey, not a destination. There will be ups and downs, but God's grace and strength will sustain you throughout. Embrace His love, rely on His power, and trust in His plan for your life – a life of wholeness, healing, and abundant joy. He is your refuge, your strength, and your ultimate source of healing.

Remember that spiritual healing is not just about emotional recovery; it's about a complete restoration of your relationship with God and a renewed sense of purpose. It's about rediscovering your identity in Christ and embracing the abundant life He offers. It's a journey of reclaiming your worth, your dignity, and your spiritual potential. It's a journey that requires courage, faith, and perseverance, but one that ultimately leads to a deeper understanding of God's love, His unwavering faithfulness, and the enduring power of His grace. The path may be challenging, but the destination – a life free from the chains of toxicity and filled with the joy and peace of Christ – is worth the journey.

Healing From Generational Trauma

The insidious nature of toxic relationships often leads to a heartbreaking cycle of repeated harm. We might find ourselves drawn to similar patterns of abuse, unconsciously recreating dynamics from our past. This isn't a sign of weakness; it's a testament to the deep-seated impact of past trauma. Understanding this cyclical nature is crucial to breaking free and establishing healthy, fulfilling relationships. Our past experiences shape our present choices, often more profoundly than we realize. The familiar sting of criticism, the subtle manipulation, even the fleeting moments of affection followed by intense withdrawal—these patterns, once deeply ingrained, can become deeply familiar and, tragically, even comforting in their predictability, despite the inherent pain.

One key element in understanding this cycle is recognizing the influence of generational trauma. Just as physical ailments can be inherited, so too can emotional and relational patterns. If we grew up witnessing unhealthy relationships – perhaps a parent consistently belittling the other, or a household dominated by fear and control – these experiences shape our understanding of what constitutes a "normal" relationship. We internalize these patterns, subtly absorbing them into our expectations and responses. This is not to excuse abusive behavior; it's to acknowledge the powerful role that upbringing plays in our relational choices. We learn relationship models by observing them in our families, and if those models are toxic, the likelihood of repeating those patterns is significantly increased. These inherited patterns might manifest in different ways, from a tendency towards codependency, where we constantly seek validation from others, to a pattern of choosing emotionally unavailable partners, mirroring the emotional distance experienced in childhood.

Consider the example of a woman who grew up in a home where her father consistently controlled her mother's finances and choices. She might unconsciously seek out partners who exert similar control, even if on a more subtle level. She might rationalize this behavior, blaming herself for her partner's actions or believing that she somehow deserves such treatment. This is a prime example of generational trauma at play—a repeated pattern of unhealthy relational dynamics passed down through generations. Another example might be a man who witnessed a parent constantly criticized and belittled. He might subconsciously attract critical partners, believing that he inherently deserves such treatment or that this is simply the nature of relationships. He may even repeat the same behaviors towards his own partners, perpetuating the cycle. The cycle isn't always apparent; it can manifest in subtle, seemingly insignificant ways, making it even more challenging to identify and address.

Breaking this cycle requires a profound self-awareness and a commitment to personal growth. The first step is identifying the patterns themselves. This often involves honest reflection, journaling, and perhaps even seeking guidance from a therapist or counselor experienced in trauma-informed care. What recurring themes emerge in your relationships? Do you find yourself consistently attracted to people with similar personality traits or relational styles? Do you notice recurring themes of control, manipulation, or emotional neglect? Recognizing these patterns is the crucial first step towards interrupting them. This self-reflection, guided by prayer and a willingness to examine your heart, is vital to understanding the roots of these patterns.

Once identified, these patterns need to be challenged and confronted. This is not a simple process; it requires courage, vulnerability, and often, a willingness to face difficult truths about ourselves and our past. This might involve confronting the pain of past experiences, accepting that we are not to blame for the unhealthy patterns we've inherited, and acknowledging the impact of generational trauma. It's a process of grieving the loss of healthy relationships we never had, and reclaiming the power to forge a new, healthier path. God's grace and mercy are essential throughout this difficult journey. His word reminds us that "He heals the brokenhearted and binds up their wounds" (Psalm 147:3). His promises of restoration and renewal are potent antidotes to the despair and hopelessness that can accompany this process. Leaning on Him through prayer, scripture study, and fellowship with other believers, becomes paramount during this time. This is not a solo journey; it requires a strong support system that understands the complexities of healing from generational trauma.

Boundaries Must Be Set

Another crucial aspect is establishing healthy boundaries. This involves learning to say "no" to behaviors that are harmful or disrespectful, and setting clear expectations for how you want to be treated in relationships. This is often a challenging process, particularly for those who have grown up in environments where boundaries were either nonexistent or routinely violated. It requires learning to assert oneself without feeling guilty or selfish, a skill that can be cultivated through counseling, support groups, and a deepening relationship with God. He empowers us to set boundaries that honor His creation and protect our well-being. His wisdom guides us to establish these parameters without resentment or judgment, focusing on establishing healthy and balanced relationships.

Furthermore, fostering healthy attachments requires actively cultivating secure relationships. This involves seeking relationships with people who respect your boundaries, value your opinions, and treat you with kindness and compassion. It means seeking out mentors, support systems, and friendships that offer a sense of belonging and unconditional love. This requires choosing wisely, recognizing that not all relationships are created equal, and selecting the ones that build you up rather than tear you down. This discernment is built through prayer and a deepening relationship with God. He provides the discernment to recognize people who offer genuine support and provides us with the strength to resist unhealthy relationships. Remember, you are not responsible for other people's choices, but you are responsible for choosing your own relationships wisely.

Finally, cultivating self-compassion is paramount. Healing from the effects of toxic relationships and generational trauma takes time and effort. There will be setbacks, moments of doubt, and times when old patterns resurface. This is a normal part of the healing process, and treating yourself with kindness and understanding is crucial during these times. Self-compassion isn't self-indulgence; it's recognizing that you're on a journey of healing and that progress is not always linear. It's remembering that God's love is unconditional, and His grace is sufficient for every challenge you face. His forgiveness extends not only to others but to yourself as well, enabling you to move forward with hope and confidence.

The journey of breaking the cycle of abuse is not easy, but it is entirely possible. With the help of God, the support of others, and a commitment to personal growth, you can create a future free from the chains of the past. Remember, your worth is inherent in Christ, regardless of the experiences you've endured. His love is unwavering, His grace is sufficient, and His power is made perfect in weakness (2 Corinthians 12:9). Embrace His healing, trust in His plan, and embark on this restoration journey with courage, faith, and hope. He promises to lead you toward a life of wholeness, joy, and abundant love, free from the destructive patterns of the past. The process will be difficult at times, demanding vulnerability and courage to confront your past and reshape your present, but remember the power of God's grace is always available. His love is transformative, and His power can break the toughest cycles. Lean into Him and allow Him to guide you towards a future filled with healthy, fulfilling relationships and the peace that surpasses all understanding.

Chapter 2

Establishing Healthy Boundaries

Understanding boundaries is crucial to navigating the complexities of life and fostering healthy relationships. A boundary, in its simplest form, is a line that defines where one person ends and another begins. It's a demarcation that protects our physical, emotional, and spiritual well-being, safeguarding us from undue influence, manipulation, or harm. Without clear boundaries, we risk being overwhelmed, exploited, or depleted by the demands and expectations of others. This can lead to resentment, burnout, and a diminished sense of self. Establishing and maintaining healthy boundaries isn't about selfishness; it's an act of self-preservation and respect, a recognition of our inherent worth and the limits of our capacity.

The Bible speaks frequently about boundaries, although not explicitly using the modern term. Proverbs 25:17 advises, "Seldom set foot in your neighbor's house—too much familiarity breeds contempt." This verse highlights the wisdom of maintaining appropriate distance in relationships to prevent over-familiarity and potential conflict. The concept of "loving your neighbor as yourself" (Matthew 22:39) implicitly involves respecting your own needs and limits, thereby preventing the blurring of lines that can lead to unhealthy dependencies. Similarly, Paul's instruction in 1 Thessalonians 4:11-12 to "aspire to live quietly, and to mind your own affairs" speaks to the importance of setting personal boundaries and avoiding unnecessary entanglements.

Healthy boundaries are not rigid walls that isolate us from others. Instead, they are flexible guidelines that allow for intimacy and connection while safeguarding our well-being. They are dynamic, adapting to the changing contexts of our lives and relationships. Think of them as a fence around a garden – it protects the precious plants within, allowing for sunlight, air, and nurturing, but preventing unwelcome intruders from damaging or destroying them.

Setting boundaries is a skill that requires courage, assertiveness, and self-awareness. It involves identifying our personal limits—physical, emotional, and spiritual—and then communicating those limits clearly and respectfully to others. This might involve saying "no" to requests that overstep our capabilities or compromise our values, setting limits on the time we spend with certain people, or establishing clear communication guidelines.

Consider the example of a woman struggling with a controlling mother who constantly calls, criticizes, and tries to dictate her life decisions. Setting healthy boundaries might involve setting specific times for phone calls, establishing firm limits on her criticism ("Mom, I appreciate your concern, but I need to make my own decisions."), and politely deflecting unwanted advice. This isn't about cutting off her mother entirely, but about protecting her own emotional well-being by establishing clear limits on the mother's behavior.

In romantic relationships, establishing boundaries is essential for maintaining healthy dynamics. This could involve setting limits on physical intimacy, defining expectations around communication and time spent together, or outlining personal boundaries concerning finances, social activities, and family matters. Healthy boundaries don't stifle affection; they create a secure space for intimacy to flourish. Without boundaries—resentment, conflict, and ultimately, relationship breakdown, can easily occur.

Boundaries are equally vital in friendships. This might involve limiting time spent with a friend who is consistently negative or demanding, establishing clear boundaries around sharing personal information, or refusing to participate in activities that compromise personal values. Healthy friendships involve mutual respect and recognition of each other's individual needs and limits.

In the workplace, setting boundaries is crucial for maintaining professional integrity and avoiding burnout. This might involve setting limits on the amount of overtime, establishing clear communication channels for work-related inquiries, or refusing to take on additional responsibilities that overload one's capacity. Setting professional boundaries doesn't mean being uncooperative, but rather safeguarding your health and preventing exploitation.

Communicating boundaries effectively is essential for their success. It requires clear, assertive communication, expressed with respect but firmness. Avoid apologetic language or passive-aggressive behaviors that can confuse or undermine the message. For instance, instead of saying, "I'm sorry, but I can't do that right now," try, "I'm not available to assist with that at this time." The difference is subtle yet significant, conveying a stronger sense of self-assurance and conviction.

It's also important to be prepared for resistance. When we set boundaries, we may encounter pushback from those who are used to controlling or manipulating us. This is where consistent firmness, yet respectful communication, is key. Reaffirming boundaries calmly and consistently demonstrates your resolve and helps others understand your limits. Avoid getting drawn into arguments or feeling the need to justify your decisions extensively.

Boundary Maintenance

Maintaining boundaries requires ongoing vigilance. It's a continuous process, not a one-time event. We may need to adjust our boundaries as our lives and relationships evolve. Regular self-reflection is key to recognizing when our boundaries are being crossed and taking steps to restore them. Regular prayer and seeking guidance from trusted friends or mentors can assist in identifying areas where we need to strengthen or adjust our boundaries.

Furthermore, recognizing the importance of self-care is crucial in maintaining healthy boundaries. Self-care involves prioritizing our physical, emotional, and spiritual well-being. This may include engaging in activities that nourish the soul, such as spending time in nature, engaging in hobbies, or pursuing spiritual practices. It also involves getting enough sleep, eating nutritious food, and exercising regularly. When prioritizing self-care, we are better equipped to establish and maintain healthy boundaries because we are less likely to be depleted or overwhelmed.

The ultimate goal of setting boundaries is not to isolate ourselves but to create healthy, fulfilling relationships where we can thrive. By establishing and maintaining healthy boundaries, we protect our well-being, foster mutual respect, and pave the way for authentic connection and growth. It is a testament to our self-worth and a reflection of our commitment to living a life aligned with God's design for us, fostering relationships rooted in mutual respect and love. Remember, setting boundaries is not selfish; it's a necessary act of self-preservation that honors both you and your relationships.

Communicating boundaries effectively is the cornerstone of healthy relationships. It's not merely about stating your limits; it's about conveying them with clarity, respect, and firmness. This involves a shift in mindset, moving away from passive-aggressive behaviors or apologetic language and towards assertive, yet compassionate communication. Think of it as a delicate balance – upholding your needs without causing unnecessary offense or conflict.

One of the most common mistakes in boundary communication is the use of apologetic language. Phrases like, "I'm sorry, but..." or "I feel bad, but..." instantly diminish the strength of your message and position you in a place of weakness. These phrases inadvertently communicate a lack of confidence in your own needs and can leave the other person feeling they can easily push back. Instead of apologizing for your needs, own them. Replace "I'm sorry, but I can't help you move this weekend" with "I won't be able to help you move this weekend." The subtle shift in wording significantly alters the perception and impact of your communication.

Similarly, passive-aggressive behaviors, such as sulking, giving the silent treatment, or making sarcastic remarks, are ineffective and often counterproductive. They create confusion and resentment rather than fostering understanding. While frustration might fuel these responses, they rarely achieve the desired outcome. Even if it is uncomfortable, direct communication is always more effective in the long run. Instead of passively withdrawing from a conversation about an unmet need, directly address the issue. For example, instead of silently avoiding phone calls from a friend who monopolizes your time, have an open and honest conversation about scheduling. "I value our friendship, but I need to set some boundaries around our phone calls so I can manage my time effectively. Perhaps we could schedule calls for shorter periods?"

Effective boundary communication requires clarity. Be specific about your limits and what constitutes a boundary violation. Vague statements invite misinterpretation and leave room for the other person to push the boundaries. For instance, saying "I need more space" is less effective than saying, "I need at least one day a week to myself to recharge, free from social engagements." The latter clearly defines the desired outcome and the actions needed to respect the boundary.

Consider this example: You have a friend who constantly calls you for lengthy conversations, often during inconvenient times. You need to establish a boundary around your time. Instead of vaguely saying, "I'm busy lately," try a more assertive approach: "Hey [Friend's name], I really appreciate our friendship and enjoy talking to you, but my schedule is tight at the moment. Could we schedule our calls for a specific timeframe, perhaps [suggested time] on [specific days]?" This approach is direct, respectful, and offers a solution, rather than just presenting a problem.

Role-playing is a powerful tool for practicing assertive communication. Imagine scenarios where your boundaries might be tested, such as a colleague asking you to work overtime on a regular basis, or a family member making insensitive comments. Practice responding assertively yet compassionately, stating your limits clearly, and offering alternatives where possible. This can help you build confidence and refine your communication skills. It is also helpful to articulate your own feelings within the boundary-setting process. Use "I" statements to describe your feelings rather than accusations or generalizations. For instance, "I feel overwhelmed when I'm constantly asked to work late" rather than "You always make me work late."

Furthermore, anticipate resistance. Setting boundaries can trigger defensiveness or anger in others, especially those accustomed to crossing those boundaries. Prepare for this possibility and develop strategies to respond calmly and firmly. Reaffirm your boundaries without escalating the conflict. Avoid getting drawn into arguments or feeling the need to constantly justify your decisions. Remember that you are not responsible for their feelings or reactions, only for clearly communicating your boundaries.

Set Boundaries, Not Walls

Maintaining boundaries is an ongoing process, not a one-time event. Your needs and circumstances will change, necessitating adjustments to your boundaries. Regular self-reflection is crucial in assessing the effectiveness of your boundaries and making necessary adjustments. Ask yourself: Are my boundaries still serving me? Are they being respected? Am I communicating them effectively? If not, don't hesitate to revise and refine your approach.

Another crucial element in boundary setting is understanding the difference between a boundary and a wall. While boundaries protect you and your well-being, a wall isolates you entirely, cutting off connections and potentially stifling healthy relationships. Boundaries allow for healthy connections while simultaneously prioritizing your own needs and well-being. A wall, on the other hand, completely shuts others out. For instance, a boundary would limit the amount of time you spend with someone who is draining; a wall would end the friendship altogether.

Consider the biblical principle of loving your neighbor as yourself. This isn't a call to be a doormat, but a call to respect your own needs as a fundamental expression of self-love. It's recognizing that caring for yourself isn't selfish; it's essential for your ability to care for others effectively. When you are depleted and overwhelmed, your capacity to love and support others is diminished. Setting boundaries is, therefore, an act of self-preservation and a prerequisite to genuinely loving others.

Finally, integrating your faith into your boundary-setting process can provide strength, guidance, and peace. Pray for wisdom and discernment as you navigate challenging relationships. Seek counsel from trusted mentors or spiritual advisors who can offer support and accountability. Remember that God equips you with the strength and resilience to establish and maintain healthy boundaries, creating space for flourishing relationships rooted in mutual respect, love, and grace. He doesn't call us to be doormats but empowers us to navigate life with strength and wisdom. Setting healthy boundaries is not a sign of weakness; it is a testament to your commitment to your own well-being and to honoring God's design for your life.

Enforcing boundaries isn't a one-time action; it's an ongoing commitment. It requires consistent vigilance and the willingness to address violations directly and compassionately. This often means facing resistance, experiencing discomfort, and navigating difficult conversations. However, the rewards for protecting your emotional, physical, and spiritual well-being far outweigh the challenges.

One of the first steps in enforcing boundaries is recognizing when they've been violated. This isn't always obvious. Sometimes, violations are subtle, manifesting as passive-aggressive behaviors, manipulative comments, or subtle disregard for your stated limits. For example, you might have established a boundary around your work hours, stating that you won't work overtime on a regular basis. A violation might be a colleague consistently asking you to stay late, even after you've explained your limits. Or perhaps a family member consistently calls late at night, even after you've asked them to respect your sleep schedule. These seemingly small infractions, if left unaddressed, erode the strength of your boundaries and ultimately invite further violations.

Responding to boundary violations requires assertive

communication, similar to the communication strategies discussed in the previous section. However, in this context, assertiveness incorporates a firmer tone and a clear indication that you will not tolerate further transgressions. It's about stating your boundary again, clearly and directly, and outlining the consequences of continued violations. This doesn't necessarily mean anger or hostility; it's about conveying a firm resolve to uphold your limits while maintaining respect for the other person.

Consider the example of a friend who consistently borrows money without repaying it, despite your previously established boundary against lending large sums. A response might be, "I've told you before that I'm not comfortable lending large amounts of money. I understand you're in a difficult situation, but I must stick to my boundary. Next time you need financial assistance, I encourage you to consider other options." This response acknowledges the friend's situation but firmly restates the boundary and its implications.

Dealing with guilt and manipulation is often a significant hurdle in enforcing boundaries. People who are used to crossing your boundaries may attempt to manipulate you into feeling guilty for upholding your limits. They might use emotional blackmail, playing on your empathy and sense of responsibility. They might say things like, "You're such a bad friend for not helping me," or "You're so selfish for not putting my needs first." These are classic manipulation tactics designed to undermine your boundaries and make you feel responsible for their feelings.

Recognizing these tactics is crucial. Remember that you are not responsible for other people's feelings or reactions. Your responsibility lies in clearly communicating your boundaries and upholding them consistently. Responding to guilt trips with assertive compassion can effectively defuse manipulation attempts. For example, you could say, "I understand you're feeling frustrated, but my decision is based on my own needs and limits, which I've clearly communicated. I care about you, but I can't let your feelings override my need to protect my own well-being."

Another crucial aspect of enforcing boundaries is understanding and accepting the potential consequences. Setting boundaries can lead to conflict, strained relationships, or even the loss of certain relationships. This is a difficult reality, but it's important to remember that healthy relationships are built on mutual respect and understanding, not on sacrificing your own well-being. Holding firm to your boundaries might lead to the distancing of those who are unwilling to respect them. While painful, this distancing can be necessary for your spiritual, emotional, and physical health. God often uses these moments to refine our trust in Him and to show us the relationships that truly align with His will.

The potential benefits of consistent boundary enforcement far outweigh the temporary discomfort. By protecting your emotional, physical, and spiritual well-being, you create space for healthier relationships, improved self-esteem, and a stronger sense of self. You'll experience reduced stress, less anxiety, and an increased capacity to love and serve others authentically. Remember, establishing healthy boundaries is an act of self-love and a demonstration of your commitment to honoring God's design for your life. It is not a sign of weakness but a testament to your spiritual maturity and your understanding of God's love and grace.

Consider the parable of the Good Samaritan. The Samaritan didn't avoid the injured man because it was inconvenient or risky; he acted out of compassion and a commitment to caring for those in need. Similarly, setting boundaries doesn't mean rejecting those who need help; it means setting realistic limits that allow you to help others without depleting yourself. It's about having the discernment to prioritize your own well-being so that you can truly love and serve others effectively.

Faith and Boundaries

Integrating faith into the process of enforcing boundaries is vital. Pray for wisdom and discernment, seeking God's guidance in navigating difficult conversations and challenging relationships. Lean on scripture for strength and comfort, remembering verses that speak to self-worth, self-care, and the importance of healthy relationships. Surround yourself with a supportive Christian community, seeking accountability and encouragement from trusted mentors or spiritual advisors.

Remember, setting and enforcing boundaries is a journey, not a destination. There will be times when you falter, when you struggle to uphold your limits, or when you question your decisions. This is normal. Don't be discouraged; view these moments as opportunities for growth and learning. Through prayer, reflection, and ongoing practice, you will grow increasingly confident and capable in protecting your well-being and building healthier, more fulfilling relationships. The journey of establishing and enforcing boundaries is a testament to your faith, a demonstration of your love for yourself, and a profound step toward experiencing God's abundant blessings in your life. Remember, you are not alone in this process. God is with you, guiding and empowering you every step of the way.

Dealing with boundary violations can be emotionally taxing, but it's a crucial aspect of maintaining healthy relationships and prioritizing your well-being. Remember, setting boundaries isn't about being selfish; it's about self-preservation and honoring God's design for your life. When a boundary is crossed, your initial reaction might be anger, frustration, or even fear. It's important to acknowledge these feelings, but not let them dictate your response. Instead, approach the situation with prayerful discernment, seeking

God's wisdom to guide your actions.

One common response to boundary violations is anger. This anger isn't necessarily sinful; it's a natural human emotion. However, it's crucial to manage this anger biblically. Ephesians 4:26 advises, "Be angry, but do not sin; do not let the sun go down on your anger." This verse doesn't condemn anger but urges us to process it constructively and avoid letting it fester. Uncontrolled anger can lead to harsh words and actions that damage relationships further. Instead of reacting impulsively, take time to pray, breathe deeply, and seek God's guidance on how to address the situation calmly and respectfully. Consider writing down your feelings to process them before engaging in conversation.

Sometimes, expressing your anger directly is necessary. However, this needs to be done with grace and firmness. 1 Peter 3:15 encourages us to always be prepared to give an answer to everyone who asks us to give the reason for the hope that you have, but do this with gentleness and respect. This means explaining calmly but firmly why the boundary was established and how its violation affected you. Focus on the behavior, not the person, using "I" statements to communicate your feelings without blaming. For instance, instead of saying, "You always ignore my requests," try, "I feel disrespected when my requests are ignored." The goal is to communicate your needs clearly and assertively while maintaining a respectful tone.

Guilt and manipulation are often employed by those with a history of violating boundaries. They may attempt to make you feel responsible for their feelings or actions. They might employ tactics like emotional blackmail, playing on your empathy and sense of responsibility. They may say things like, "You're such a bad friend for not helping me," or "You're being selfish by prioritizing your needs." These are designed to undermine your boundaries and make you question your decisions.

Recognizing these manipulation tactics is crucial. Remember that you are not responsible for other people's feelings or reactions. Your responsibility is to protect your well-being and communicate your boundaries effectively. Responding with assertive compassion can diffuse such attempts. For example, you might say, "I understand you're feeling frustrated, but my decision is based on my own needs and limits, which I've clearly communicated. I care about you, but I can't let your feelings override my need to protect my well-being." This response acknowledges their feelings without compromising your boundaries. It emphasizes your care for them while firmly asserting your right to maintain your limits.

Another common response to boundary violations is fear. Fear of conflict, loss of relationships, or even retaliation can prevent you from upholding your boundaries. However, fear should not dictate your actions. Proverbs 29:25 states, "The fear of man lays a snare, but whoever trusts in the Lord is safe." This verse reminds us that putting our trust in God, rather than fearing others, brings safety and peace. God is with you in every situation, guiding and protecting you. Pray for courage and strength to communicate your boundaries effectively, even when it's difficult. Remember that God is your refuge and strength, a very present help in trouble (Psalm 46:1).

Remember that setting boundaries is a continuous process, not a one-time event. Expect that there will be times when you will need to reiterate your boundaries. This isn't a sign of weakness but a testament to your commitment to your well-being. It demonstrates your spiritual maturity and understanding of the importance of protecting your emotional, spiritual, and physical health. Consider keeping a journal to track your boundary enforcement and to reflect on your experiences. This can help you to see patterns and improve your approach over time. Write down how you felt before, during, and after a boundary enforcement interaction, and analyze what worked and what could be improved.

Maintaining healthy boundaries doesn't mean isolating yourself from others. It means choosing mutually respectful and supportive relationships. It's about surrounding yourself with people who value and honor your limits. These relationships will nourish your soul rather than deplete it. Remember that God calls us to love and serve others, but not at the expense of our own well-being. This means being discerning about the relationships we cultivate and the energy we invest in them.

The Bible offers many examples of setting and enforcing boundaries. Jesus himself often withdrew from crowds to pray and recharge (Mark 1:35). He knew the importance of solitude and spiritual renewal. Joseph's story highlights the importance of protecting oneself from temptation. He resisted Potiphar's wife's advances, clearly establishing a boundary against sexual immorality (Genesis 39). These biblical examples illustrate that setting boundaries is not inconsistent with love and faith, but rather essential for living a life that honors God.

Ultimately, dealing with boundary violations requires a combination of assertiveness, compassion, and faith. Remember to pray for wisdom and guidance throughout the process. Lean on scripture for strength and comfort, and surround yourself with a supportive community that will uphold you in your efforts. It's a journey of learning, growing, and prioritizing your well-being – a journey that is well worth the effort. The blessings that come from setting and maintaining healthy boundaries are immense – stronger relationships, increased self-esteem, and a deeper connection with God. This is a testament to your faith, a demonstration of your self-love, and a significant step toward living a life that truly honors

God's will. Remember, God is always with you, empowering you each step of the way. Embrace the journey with courage, faith, and unwavering trust in His plan for your life.

Firmness and Empathy

Maintaining boundaries within the context of difficult family relationships and close friendships presents unique challenges. The emotional ties and ingrained patterns of interaction can make enforcing boundaries feel particularly daunting. However, it's crucial to remember that your well-being is paramount, and setting boundaries, even within these intricate relationships, is not an act of selfishness but an act of self-preservation rooted in biblical principles. God calls us to love others, but this love should never come at the expense of our own mental, emotional, or spiritual health.

One of the key distinctions in maintaining boundaries within difficult relationships lies in the need for a delicate balance between firmness and compassion. While assertiveness remains vital, it needs to be tempered with an understanding of the complexities involved. For example, a family member struggling with addiction might react defensively when confronted with a boundary regarding their behavior. In such cases, responding with anger or judgment will likely worsen the situation. Instead, try approaching the situation with a combination of empathy and firmness. You might say something like, "Mom, I love you deeply, and I'm concerned about your well-being. I understand that addiction is a difficult struggle, but I can't allow myself to be drawn into enabling behaviors. Therefore, I will not be available to lend money or cover up any negative consequences of your actions. This isn't about rejecting you; it's about protecting myself and setting healthy limits." This approach acknowledges the person's struggles while clearly communicating the boundary and its rationale.

In dealing with close friendships, boundary maintenance often requires similar tact. A friend who consistently overshares or seeks constant emotional support might resent the setting of limits. However, it's important to remember that you are not responsible for carrying the emotional burdens of others. You can offer support and compassion, but you must also protect your own energy and well-being. You could gently explain, "Sarah, I value our friendship immensely, but I've realized I need to prioritize my own mental space. While I'm always here to listen to and support you, I need to limit our conversations to a reasonable time frame. I hope you understand this is not a reflection on our friendship, but a necessary step for me to manage my own stress levels effectively. Perhaps we can schedule some dedicated time for our conversations."

Navigating family dynamics often necessitates understanding the generational differences in communication styles and expectations. Older generations might view boundary setting as disrespectful or disobedient, particularly if they are accustomed to more enmeshed family relationships. In such situations, patience and clear communication are key. It's important to explain your reasons for setting boundaries calmly and respectfully, emphasizing that it's not about rejecting them but about protecting your well-being. You may even need to educate them about healthy boundaries and their importance in maintaining balanced relationships.

Consider situations involving manipulative family members. They might use guilt trips, emotional blackmail, or subtle forms of coercion to manipulate you into ignoring your boundaries. For example, an overly critical parent might use phrases like, "You're so selfish for not doing this for me," or "After everything I've done for you…" In such scenarios, it's crucial to identify the manipulative tactics and respond with assertiveness. You might say, "Mom, I understand you feel this way, but I'm setting this boundary for my own well-being, and I need you to respect that. I love you, and I'm happy to help where I can, but I can't let myself be manipulated into feeling guilty for prioritizing my needs."

Self-care is an integral component of maintaining boundaries in difficult relationships. It's easy to become depleted when dealing with constant demands and emotional manipulation. Therefore, prioritize activities that replenish your emotional and spiritual reserves. This might involve spending time in prayer, meditating on scripture, engaging in hobbies, or spending time in nature. Remember that you cannot pour from an empty cup. Taking care of your own well-being is not selfish; it's essential to effectively set and maintain boundaries. Make sure to schedule dedicated time for self-care and stick to that schedule. Consider this as an appointment you cannot miss.

Remember that forgiveness is a powerful tool in navigating difficult relationships. Holding onto resentment and bitterness only fuels negativity and prevents healing. Forgiving those who violate your boundaries does not mean condoning their behavior; it means releasing the anger and bitterness that hold you captive. Forgiveness allows you to move forward and maintain healthy emotional detachment. It allows you to focus on your well-being and moving forward constructively. This doesn't require condoning the behavior. It is about releasing the burden of negativity and resentment. Remember that extending forgiveness can be a deeply spiritual act and a source of personal healing and emotional release.

Maintaining boundaries in challenging relationships requires ongoing effort and vigilance. You will likely experience setbacks and moments of doubt, and that is perfectly normal. Don't get discouraged by setbacks; view them as opportunities for growth and refinement. Reflect on the situations, identify what worked and what didn't, and adjust your approach accordingly. Journaling, therapy, or accountability groups can provide valuable support during this process. A support system of trusted friends or family members who understand and respect your boundaries can offer encouragement and guidance when needed.

Remember, the goal is not to isolate yourself from these relationships entirely, but to reshape them into healthier and more balanced interactions. It's about creating space for genuine connection and mutual respect, where your needs are honored, and your well-being is not compromised. It's a process that takes time and patience, but the rewards – increased self-esteem, improved emotional health, and stronger, more authentic relationships – are immeasurable. Ultimately, maintaining healthy boundaries in difficult relationships is a testament to your self-respect and a demonstration of your faith in God's ability to guide and protect you. It's a spiritual discipline that leads to greater emotional freedom and spiritual maturity, reflecting the love and grace you find in Christ. This process will bring about a deeper connection with God and a greater sense of self-worth. Remember to trust in His plan for your life. He will guide you through the challenging times and help you find the strength you need to navigate these relationships constructively.

Chapter 3

Healing From Past Trauma

Understanding trauma's impact is crucial for healing. Trauma, in its broadest sense, refers to deeply distressing or disturbing experiences that overwhelm an individual's ability to cope. These experiences can range from single, catastrophic events like accidents or natural disasters to prolonged periods of abuse, neglect, or chronic instability. The defining characteristic of trauma isn't the event itself, but rather the individual's response to it. If an experience leaves someone feeling profoundly helpless, terrified, or violated, it can have lasting effects, even decades later. It's not merely a matter of "getting over it." The emotional scars of trauma run deep, subtly yet powerfully shaping how we navigate the world and our relationships.

The physical manifestations of trauma can be surprisingly varied and sometimes subtle. Chronic pain, unexplained aches, digestive issues, and sleep disturbances are common. These physical symptoms often arise from the body's prolonged state of hyper-vigilance, a survival mechanism triggered by past trauma. The body remains on high alert, even when there's no immediate threat, leading to muscular tension, increased heart rate, and other physiological changes that contribute to chronic discomfort. Headaches, migraines, and even autoimmune disorders can be linked to unresolved trauma. These physical symptoms often go unnoticed or misdiagnosed, delaying the healing process. Understanding this connection is critical for healing.

Emotional manifestations of trauma are often more readily apparent, yet equally complex. Many survivors experience persistent feelings of anxiety, fear, and sadness. Flashbacks, nightmares, and intrusive thoughts related to the traumatic event are common. These can significantly impact daily life, making it challenging to focus, sleep soundly, or maintain healthy relationships. The sense of being constantly "on edge" is characteristic, leading to difficulty relaxing and enjoying life's simple pleasures. Low self-esteem and a sense of shame are also frequent companions of trauma, stemming from feelings of helplessness and powerlessness during the traumatic experience. Individuals might struggle to trust others or develop healthy attachments, fearing a repetition of past hurts.

Trauma's impact extends far beyond these individual symptoms; it profoundly shapes how individuals interact with their world and, particularly, their relationships. Difficulties with intimacy are common. The inability to trust others fully can make it incredibly challenging to form close, meaningful connections. The constant fear of betrayal or abandonment, rooted in past experiences, can lead to emotional distance and avoidance of vulnerability. This can manifest in various ways, from difficulty expressing emotions to a persistent sense of detachment in otherwise intimate situations. Fear of intimacy can inadvertently push others away, perpetuating a cycle of isolation and reinforcing the feeling of being unsafe.

In romantic relationships, trauma can lead to patterns of codependency or unhealthy attachment styles. Survivors might unconsciously seek out partners who mirror the abusive or neglectful dynamics of their past, perpetuating the cycle of trauma. This can manifest as a desperate need for approval, a reluctance to assert personal boundaries, or a tendency to tolerate unhealthy behaviors in a partner. Conversely, some survivors may adopt an avoidant attachment style, fearing intimacy and pushing potential partners away before genuine connection can occur. Both styles stem from a deep-seated need for control and safety, born from past experiences of helplessness and lack of control.

The impact of trauma on friendships can be equally significant. Trauma survivors may struggle to maintain healthy friendships, either by pushing others away to protect themselves or by becoming overly reliant on friends for emotional support, blurring boundaries and creating unhealthy dependencies. Trust issues may lead to a reluctance to fully open up to friends, creating barriers to genuine connection. This can lead to feelings of loneliness and isolation, even when surrounded by people. Friendships built on a foundation of unspoken trauma can be inherently unbalanced, leaving one party feeling burdened and the other feeling unsupported and unheard.

Family relationships are particularly susceptible to the ripple effect of trauma. Unresolved trauma can impact parenting styles, leading to inconsistent discipline, emotional neglect, or even abuse. Children raised in homes marked by trauma may experience difficulties forming secure attachments with their parents and siblings, resulting in complex family dynamics and lingering emotional wounds. Adult children of trauma survivors might find themselves carrying the burden of their parents' unresolved trauma, unknowingly replicating patterns of behavior and communication learned in childhood. Family therapy can be invaluable in unraveling these complex dynamics and promoting healing for all involved.

Recognizing the impact of past trauma on current relationships and behaviors is a crucial first step toward healing. This requires self-reflection and a willingness to confront painful memories and emotions. Keeping a journal can be a powerful tool for processing these experiences. Writing down your thoughts and feelings, reflecting on patterns in your relationships, and identifying triggers related to your trauma can offer invaluable insight. Therapy, either individually or in a group setting, can provide a safe and supportive environment to explore these issues with a trained professional.

There are several practical steps that you can take to begin the healing process. One is engaging in self-compassion. This involves treating yourself with the same kindness and understanding you would offer a close friend facing similar challenges. Acknowledge that your feelings and reactions are valid and that healing takes time and patience. Self-care is paramount. Engage in activities that nourish your mind, body, and spirit. This could involve exercise, meditation, spending time in nature, pursuing creative hobbies, or simply engaging in activities that bring you joy. Prioritizing self-care is not selfish; it's a crucial act of self-preservation and a necessary component of the healing journey.

Another essential step is cultivating a support system. Seek out trusted friends, family members, or faith-based community members who can provide empathy, understanding, and encouragement. Sharing your experiences can be empowering, helping you to feel less alone and more connected to others. Joining a support group specifically designed for trauma survivors can be particularly beneficial, providing a sense of community and a safe space to share your experiences with those who understand what you're going through. The shared experience offers a powerful sense of validation and hope.

Remember the power of forgiveness. Forgiveness is not about condoning harmful behavior; it's about releasing the burden of resentment and anger that can hold you captive. Forgiving those who have hurt you, even if they never apologize, can be a profoundly liberating act that allows you to move forward and focus on your healing. Forgiveness is ultimately an act of self-compassion; it sets you free from the chains of past hurts, allowing you to embrace a future free from the lingering bitterness and pain. This process can be incredibly challenging, and seeking guidance from a therapist or spiritual advisor can provide invaluable support.

Finally, remember your faith. Turn to your spiritual beliefs and practices as a source of strength and comfort. Lean on your faith community for support and guidance. Many find solace and healing in prayer, meditation, and engaging in spiritual practices that connect them to a higher power. Remember that God's love is unconditional, and His grace is sufficient for every challenge you face. Trust in His healing power and His unwavering support. The path to healing from trauma is not always easy, but with faith, patience, and self-compassion, you can find freedom and hope for a brighter future. It is a journey of faith and self-discovery, and ultimately, a testament to the resilience of the human spirit. God's grace is sufficient for the journey, and His love will carry you through.

Forgiveness: The Unlocking of Healing's Door

The journey of healing from past trauma is a deeply personal and often arduous one. While acknowledging the pain, understanding its roots, and engaging in self-care are crucial steps, there remains a powerful key that often unlocks the final chambers of emotional freedom: forgiveness. This isn't a simplistic act of forgetting or condoning the actions of those who caused us harm. Instead, forgiveness is a profound act of releasing the bitterness, anger, and resentment that bind us to our past, allowing us to step into a future unburdened by the weight of past hurts.

It's vital to understand the distinction between forgiveness and condoning. Forgiving someone does not mean we approve of their actions or minimize the harm they inflicted. It doesn't mean we invite them back into our lives or erase the boundaries we've established to protect ourselves. Forgiveness is, instead, a conscious decision to release the power that these past actions have over our present emotional state. It's about surrendering the control that resentment holds, relinquishing the constant replay of painful memories that keep us tethered to the past. It's a choice to free ourselves from the chains of bitterness that prevent us from moving forward.

The process of forgiveness is rarely instantaneous; it's a journey, not a destination. It often involves several stages, including acknowledging the hurt, allowing ourselves to feel the anger and resentment without judgment, and gradually letting go of the need to control the outcome. Some find it helpful to journal their feelings and write down their anger, pain, and any unresolved issues. This process of releasing pent-up emotions onto paper can be surprisingly therapeutic, facilitating emotional release and clarity.

Consider this scenario: A woman spent years enduring emotional abuse in her marriage, silently enduring constant criticism and belittlement. The pain was deep, leaving scars on her self-esteem and trust in others. While she ultimately left the marriage, the emotional wounds lingered, fueling resentment and anger toward her former husband. She might find solace in writing about these experiences, expressing her hurt and anger without restraint. This process of emotional catharsis can pave the way for forgiveness. The journal doesn't need to be a work of art; it's simply a space for raw honesty.

Prayerful Forgiveness

Another valuable tool in the forgiveness process is prayer. Turning to God in prayer allows us to release our hurts and burdens onto Him. It's an act of surrendering our pain to a power greater than ourselves, acknowledging that we cannot control the actions of others, but we can surrender our own emotional state to God's care. Prayer is not about demanding retribution or punishment for those who have wronged us; it's about asking for God's healing grace and strength to let go of the resentment that is keeping us trapped.

The Bible offers numerous examples of forgiveness, providing guidance and hope for our own journeys. In the Lord's Prayer, Jesus instructs us to "Forgive us our trespasses, as we forgive those who trespass against us." (Matthew 6:12) This isn't a mere suggestion; it's a crucial element of our relationship with God. Our capacity to forgive others mirrors our receptiveness to God's forgiveness of our own shortcomings. To deny forgiveness to others is essentially to deny ourselves the same grace from God. The parable of the unforgiving servant (Matthew 18:23-35) powerfully illustrates the consequences of withholding forgiveness, highlighting the devastating cycle of unforgiveness and the importance of extending grace, just as we've received it.

Joseph's story in Genesis provides a striking illustration of forgiveness in the face of profound betrayal. Betrayed and sold into slavery by his own brothers, Joseph experienced immense suffering and injustice. Yet, when his brothers eventually came before him, humbled and repentant, Joseph extended forgiveness, demonstrating remarkable compassion and love. His forgiveness wasn't a simple act of forgetting; it was a powerful testament to the transformative power of grace. He recognized the hand of God in his suffering and the opportunity for reconciliation and restoration. His example showcases the immeasurable power of forgiveness to overcome deep-seated wounds and create opportunities for healing and restoration.

David's life also presents a complex tapestry of forgiveness and reconciliation. His sin with Bathsheba and subsequent actions resulted in devastating consequences for himself and others. Yet, through repentance and seeking God's forgiveness, David found restoration. His psalms often express deep sorrow for his actions, and his subsequent life demonstrates the transformative power of acknowledging sin and seeking forgiveness. He wasn't exempt from the repercussions of his actions. Still, his journey toward repentance and God's merciful forgiveness provides a potent example of the transformative power of faith and the redemptive nature of forgiveness.

The forgiveness process may also involve confronting the individuals who have caused us harm. This isn't always feasible or safe, and it's important to prioritize our own well-being. However, for some, a direct conversation can facilitate closure and healing. This conversation is not about seeking an apology or justification; it's about expressing our feelings and setting boundaries, asserting our worth and dignity. The goal is not to re-open old wounds but to acknowledge the past and take control of the narrative. It's about stating our truth and reclaiming our power. The outcome of such a conversation might not be an immediate resolution; it might even be unexpected. The key is to reclaim our personal narrative and choose a pathway forward, independently of the other person's response.

Forgiveness, ultimately, is an act of self-love. It's about releasing ourselves from resentment and anger, allowing us to move forward in peace. It is an essential act of self-compassion, freeing ourselves from the prison of the past and embracing the possibilities of the future. It's about choosing to break the cycle of bitterness and pain, and stepping into a space where healing can truly begin. The journey toward forgiveness is often complex, requiring patience, self-compassion, and the willingness to face difficult emotions. It's a testament to the resilience of the human spirit and the transformative power of God's grace. This journey is possible with faith, guidance, and support. It is a journey toward wholeness, a path illuminated by the grace of God and the enduring strength of the human spirit. The process isn't about erasing the past; it's about reclaiming our present and empowering our future. Forgiveness is the key, not to forgetting, but to healing. It unlocks the door to a future where peace, freedom, and joy are not just possibilities, but realities.

Seeking professional help is not a sign of weakness; it's a testament to your courage and commitment to your well-being. Many individuals, even those deeply rooted in faith, struggle with the idea of seeking professional help for emotional or mental health challenges. A common misconception is that seeking therapy somehow indicates a lack of faith or an inability to rely on God. This couldn't be further from the truth. God, in his infinite wisdom and compassion, provides us with various avenues for healing and growth, and professional therapeutic support is often one of those avenues.

Think of your physical health: if you were experiencing a severe physical ailment, you wouldn't hesitate to seek medical attention from a qualified doctor. Your mental and emotional health deserve the same level of care and attention. Just as a doctor can provide expert medical care, a therapist can offer valuable support and guidance in navigating the complexities of emotional and mental health. There is no shame in seeking professional help when you're struggling; it's a wise and proactive step towards healing and wholeness.

The Bible speaks extensively about caring for our entire being—body, mind, and spirit. While faith is the cornerstone of our healing journey, it doesn't negate the need for professional help when dealing with trauma. God often works through others to bring about healing. A therapist can provide a safe and confidential space to explore your experiences, process your emotions, and develop healthy coping mechanisms. They can offer tools and techniques that complement your faith, helping you integrate your spiritual beliefs with your emotional healing journey.

Finding the right therapist is crucial. It's a personal choice, and the ideal therapist will be someone with whom you feel comfortable and safe. If you identify as a Christian, you might prefer to find a therapist who shares your faith. A faith-based therapist can integrate biblical principles and spiritual practices into your treatment plan, creating a overall approach to healing that aligns with your worldview. However, even a secular therapist can offer valuable support, providing a space for you to process your emotions and develop healthy coping mechanisms.

Numerous resources are available to help you find a Christian therapist or counselor. You can start by searching online directories that allow you to filter by faith-based orientation. Additionally, many churches and Christian organizations maintain lists of recommended counselors and therapists. Your pastor or church leaders can also provide valuable guidance and referrals, connecting you with professionals who understand the specific needs of their congregation.

Before committing to a therapist, it's helpful to have an initial consultation. This allows you to get a feel for their approach, personality, and whether you feel a sense of connection and trust. Don't hesitate to ask questions during the consultation—inquire about their experience with trauma, their therapeutic approach, and their understanding of faith-based perspectives.

Support groups, both online and in-person, can also offer invaluable support. These groups provide a safe space to connect with others who have shared similar experiences, fostering a sense of community and mutual understanding. Sharing your experiences with others who understand can be profoundly therapeutic, reminding you that you are not alone in your journey. Christian support groups, in particular, can offer spiritual encouragement and a sense of fellowship during challenging times.

Remember, choosing a therapist is about finding the right fit for *you*. It's perfectly acceptable to try different therapists until you find one with whom you feel comfortable and supported. The therapeutic relationship is a collaborative one; it requires trust, open communication, and mutual respect. Choosing the right therapeutic environment is crucial.

One aspect often overlooked is the financial side of therapy. The cost of therapy can be a significant barrier for some. It's important to inquire about payment options and insurance coverage upfront. Many therapists offer sliding-scale fees, tailoring their rates to your financial situation. Exploring options like telehealth can also reduce travel costs and make therapy more accessible. Additionally, some faith-based organizations provide financial assistance for those seeking therapeutic care.

Healing Takes Time

The journey of healing from past trauma takes time, patience, and persistence. There will be setbacks and challenges along the way; it's not a linear path. However, with faith, professional support, and a commitment to self-care, you can find healing and restoration. Embracing the healing journey demonstrates courage, faith, and the recognition that your well-being is a priority. It is vital to remember that God is your constant companion through this process. His love, grace, and strength sustain you throughout this journey.

Remember the parable of the Good Samaritan (Luke 10:25-37). Though not of the same faith or social standing as the injured traveler, the Samaritan demonstrated profound compassion and care. He went beyond mere sympathy; he actively helped the injured man, providing practical assistance. This parable illustrates God's heart for us—a heart of compassion and active involvement in our healing. God uses people, including therapists and support groups, to be his hands and feet in extending his love and healing grace. Seeking professional help is not a rejection of faith but an act of faith, trusting in God's provision and accepting his help through various channels.

The decision to seek professional help is a significant step towards reclaiming your life and finding lasting peace. It is a testament to your courage and your commitment to healing. It is an affirmation of your self-worth and your desire to live a full and abundant life, the life God intended for you. Remember, your well-being matters deeply to God, and he desires to guide you on this journey of healing and wholeness. Remember to pray for guidance, seek support from your faith community, and actively participate in the therapeutic process. Your journey toward healing is a testament to God's unwavering love and grace. Through professional support and divine intervention, you can find hope and restoration.

This journey is not a solitary one; you are not alone in this process. God walks alongside you, offering his unwavering love, grace, and strength. Lean on him, trust his plan for your life, and know he desires your healing and wholeness. The path to healing is not always easy, but the destination – a life filled with peace, joy, and freedom – is worth the journey. Embrace the opportunities for growth and healing that lie ahead. Remember, you are valued, you are loved, and you are worthy of healing. The journey might be long, but with faith, perseverance, and the right support system, healing is not only possible, but a promise waiting to be fulfilled. The power of God's love and grace can work miracles in your life.

Let's consider specific examples. Imagine Sarah, a devout Christian woman, struggling with anxiety after a difficult divorce. She might feel conflicted about seeking therapy, fearing judgment or a perception of weakness within her faith community. However, understanding that seeking professional help is a sign of strength, not weakness, allows her to overcome this barrier and seek the assistance she needs. A skilled therapist, sensitive to her faith, can help Sarah navigate her anxiety, providing coping strategies and spiritual guidance to integrate her faith into her healing journey. Sarah will find that the therapeutic process complements her spiritual life, not replaces it.

Similarly, consider John, a man grappling with the aftermath of childhood trauma. He might harbor deep-seated shame and guilt, hesitant to share his experiences with others, even within his church community. However, through prayer and seeking guidance from trusted spiritual leaders, he discovers that sharing his story can be part of his healing journey. He finds a Christian counselor who helps him process his trauma in a safe and supportive environment, fostering a deeper understanding of God's healing love and grace.

These are but two examples of many. The healing journey is unique and personal, tailored to the individual's specific circumstances, spiritual beliefs, and past experiences. It's a journey of self-discovery, reconciliation, and transformation, guiding you toward a life of wholeness, purpose, and joy in Christ. The process is not about quick fixes or superficial solutions, but rather about embarking on a path of deep healing and transformative growth.

Each step taken is a step closer towards the restoration that God promises.

Remember, healing is a process, not an event. It will likely involve ups and downs, moments of progress and setbacks. However, by embracing faith, professional support, and a commitment to self-care, you can navigate the challenges and emerge stronger, healthier, and more resilient. Maintaining open communication with your therapist and any support systems you have in place is crucial. It is a testament to your commitment to your own well-being and spiritual growth. God is always with you, providing strength, guidance, and comfort as you embark on this journey toward healing and wholeness. He desires your healing and will walk with you every step of the way. Trust in his love, grace, and power.

The journey toward healing from past trauma is not solely dependent on professional help and support groups; it necessitates a overall approach that integrates self-care and spiritual practices. These practices aren't merely add-ons; they are fundamental pillars supporting the entire healing process. They provide the internal strength and resilience necessary to navigate the emotional complexities of trauma and emerge stronger on the other side. Think of them as the internal scaffolding, strengthening your inner structure while the external support systems—therapy and support groups—provide external bracing. Together, they create a strong foundation for lasting healing.

Cornerstone of Faith

Prayer, a cornerstone of the Christian faith, is far more than a mere request for assistance. It's a profound act of communion with God, a conversation where we pour out our hearts, share our vulnerabilities, and receive solace and strength. In the context of trauma healing, prayer becomes a lifeline, a space to express emotions that are too difficult to articulate otherwise. It's an avenue for surrender, allowing God to carry the weight of your pain and offer comfort amidst the storm. It's about relinquishing control, acknowledging that we are not alone in our suffering, and placing our trust in a higher power who understands and cares deeply.

There is no right or wrong way to pray. What truly matters is that your prayer comes from the heart. Speak to God as you would to a trusted friend. Be sincere in what you say. Sincerity plays a significant role in receiving answers. Hebrews 10:22-23 tells us: "Let us draw near with a true heart in full assurance of faith, having our hearts sprinkled from an evil conscience and our bodies washed with pure water. Let us hold fast to the profession of our faith without wavering, for He is faithful who promised." God is faithful and will answer if you believe.

Meditation, often associated with Eastern practices, also holds significant value in Christian healing. It's a disciplined practice of focusing on a specific object, thought, or sensation, quieting the mind's incessant chatter. In a Christian context, this focus can be directed toward scripture verses, listening to worship music, or simply the presence of God. Through regular meditation, you can cultivate a sense of inner peace, manage stress more effectively, and develop greater emotional regulation.

The benefits of meditation extend far beyond stress reduction. It can help to unravel the tangled threads of trauma, allowing you to observe your emotions without being overwhelmed by them. This mindful awareness fosters emotional resilience, enabling you to respond to challenging situations with greater composure and clarity. By quieting the noise of the mind, you create space for the gentle whispers of God's guidance and healing presence. Consider guided Christian meditations, readily available online or through apps, to assist you in this practice.

Journaling offers another powerful tool for emotional processing. Writing down your thoughts and feelings can provide a cathartic release, helping to untangle the complexities of your trauma. It's a private space where you can explore your emotions without judgment, allowing you to confront your pain in a safe and controlled environment. Journaling doesn't have to be a chore; it can be a creative outlet, a way to express yourself through words, poetry, or even art.

The act of writing itself can be therapeutic. It allows you to externalize your emotions, providing a sense of distance and perspective. Through journaling, you can identify patterns in your thinking and behavior, gain insights into your triggers, and track your progress in the healing process. Reflecting on scripture passages or inspirational quotes within your journal can further enhance your spiritual growth and provide guidance and hope.

Physical activity, often overlooked in the context of emotional healing, plays a vital role in overall well-being. Exercise releases endorphins, natural mood boosters that alleviate stress and anxiety. It's a healthy way to channel pent-up energy and emotions, promoting both physical and emotional health. Whether it's a brisk walk in nature, a yoga session, or a vigorous workout at the gym, engaging in regular physical activity can significantly enhance your healing journey.

The physical act of movement can be deeply therapeutic. It's a way to connect with your body, ground yourself in the present moment, and release the tension held within. Exercise can be a powerful form of self-care, providing a sense of accomplishment and self-efficacy and bolstering resilience in the face of adversity. Remember to listen to your body and choose activities that you find enjoyable and sustainable.

Incorporating these self-care and spiritual practices into your daily routine is crucial. Start small, focusing on one or two practices at a time, gradually integrating them into your daily rhythm. Consistency is key; even a few minutes each day can make a significant difference over time. Create a self-care plan, scheduling specific times for prayer, meditation, journaling, or physical activity, just as you would schedule other important appointments.

Consider creating a quiet space in your home, a sanctuary where you can retreat for prayer and meditation. Keep a journal handy, making it easy to jot down your thoughts and feelings throughout the day. Schedule regular exercise, perhaps integrating it with time in nature for added therapeutic benefits. Make these practices a non-negotiable part of your daily routine, as vital as eating healthy and getting sufficient sleep.

Remember, your healing journey is a marathon, not a sprint. There will be days when you feel strong and empowered, and days when you feel overwhelmed and discouraged. Be patient and compassionate with yourself. Celebrate your progress, no matter how small, and acknowledge setbacks as opportunities for growth. Continue to lean on your faith, your support system, and your self-care practices, knowing that God is walking alongside you every step of the way.

Integrating these self-care practices and spiritual disciplines isn't about adding more to an already burdened life; it's about prioritizing your well-being, recognizing that you are a precious child of God deserving of care and attention. It's about recognizing that true healing is an all-encompassing process that nourishes your body, mind, and spirit. It's a journey of self-discovery, self-compassion, and profound connection with your Creator. Embrace this journey with faith, hope, and the unwavering belief that restoration and wholeness are within your reach. The path may be challenging, but the destination—a life filled with peace, joy, and freedom in Christ—is worth the effort. Remember, your healing is a testament to God's love and grace, a reflection of His transformative power in your life.

The journey to healing from past trauma goes beyond just relying on professional help and support groups. It embraces a natural approach that lovingly weaves in self-care and spiritual practices. These practices are not just extras but essential pillars that uphold the healing process. They offer the inner strength and resilience you need to navigate the emotional ups and downs of trauma, helping you emerge even stronger on the other side. Consider them as the wonderful internal scaffolding that strengthens your inner self, while the external support systems—such as therapy and supportive groups—offer valuable assistance. Together, they create a solid foundation for enduring healing.

Let's not forget that prayer transcends a simple call for help. It serves as a deep communion with God—a dialogue where we express our innermost feelings, reveal our vulnerabilities, and find reassurance and strength. During trauma healing, prayer acts as a vital resource, creating a safe space to release emotions that are often hard to express. It provides an opportunity for surrender, enabling God to bear the burden of our pain and deliver comfort amid chaos. This process involves letting go of control, recognizing that we are not solitary in our suffering, and trusting an empathetic higher power that truly understands our struggles.

There are so many wonderful ways to pray, each with its own beautiful purpose! Intercessory prayer, where you lift up others or seek healing for yourself, can really strengthen your bond with others and give you a true sense of meaning. Confessional prayer, where you share your struggles with God, can feel incredibly freeing, helping you let go of any guilt or shame you may carry.

Gratitude prayer, which focuses on the blessings in your life, helps nurture a positive outlook and builds resilience in your journey. And then there's contemplative prayer, a gentle, quiet time spent in communion with God, inviting you to reflect and deepen your spiritual connection. So go ahead and explore these different forms of prayer to discover what speaks to your heart and brings you the most peace!

Incorporating daily meditation on God's word is a vital aspect of spiritual growth and self-discovery. By dedicating time each day to read and reflect on the Scriptures, you can develop a profound understanding of your intrinsic worth and the unique purpose for which you were created. This practice not only fosters a closer relationship with God but also illuminates the path toward realizing your potential and embracing the identity intended by the Creator. Through this exploration of biblical teachings, we are reminded of our value and the meaningful roles we play in the world.

This mindful awareness doesn't just help you recognize your emotions; it actively fosters emotional resilience. Picture yourself confronting life's challenges—whether they're work-related pressures, personal conflicts, or everyday frustrations—with a newfound sense of composure and mental clarity. As you quiet the incessant chatter of your mind, you'll create a serene environment that allows for the gentle, guiding whispers of God's presence to permeate your thoughts, providing comfort and insight.

Journaling Your Healing Process

As I've mentioned before, Journaling is an exceptionally transformative practice that can significantly aid in your healing journey. By taking the time to write down your thoughts and feelings, you can begin to unravel the tangled web of emotions that often accompany trauma. Each written word serves as a release, offering you an opportunity to reflect on your experiences, fears, and hopes in a private and safe environment.

As you pour your heart onto the pages, you create a sacred space where you are free to explore your innermost thoughts without judgment. This process not only helps you gain clarity about your feelings but also provides a poignant outlet for your pain, anger, and confusion. It can feel as if the weight of your burdens is being lifted with each entry, transforming your experiences into narratives that empower you to heal and grow. Embrace the journey of self-discovery that journaling offers; it can be a powerful catalyst for profound emotional healing.

Transform your life by incorporating more physical activity into your routine! Consider taking a leisurely walk in your neighborhood park, where you can enjoy the fresh air and the beauty of nature around you. Alternatively, dedicate some time to volunteering at a local animal shelter, where you can make a significant impact on the lives of abandoned pets while also gaining companionship and joy from their playful energy.

Another excellent option is to enroll in an exercise program that excites you—whether it's yoga, dance, or martial arts. These classes not only keep you physically active but also offer a wonderful way to meet new people and foster a sense of community.

Actively engaging in these pursuits is crucial for your emotional health. Instead of getting trapped in the cycle of negative thoughts and past trauma, focus on the empowering benefits of movement and connection. You'll discover that taking these steps can help lift your spirits, boost your mood, and lead you toward a more positive and fulfilling life.

Incorporating these self-care and spiritual practices into your daily routine is crucial. Start small, focusing on one or two practices at a time, gradually integrating them into your daily rhythm. Consistency is key; even a few minutes each day can make a significant difference over time. Create a self-care plan, scheduling specific times for prayer, meditation, journaling, or physical activity, just as you would schedule other important appointments.

Consider creating a quiet space in your home, a sanctuary where you can retreat for prayer and meditation. Keep a journal handy, making it easy to jot down your thoughts and feelings throughout the day. Schedule regular exercise, perhaps integrating it with time in nature for added therapeutic benefits. Make these practices a non-negotiable part of your daily routine, as vital as eating healthy and getting sufficient sleep.

Don't let the speed of your transformation dishearten you. There will be days when progress feels slow, and on these days, it's easy to question your journey. However, each of those slower days contributes to your overall growth, just as much as the days when you feel a surge of motivation and energy. It's important to take time to celebrate your achievements, no matter their size. Whether you've completed a major goal or taken a small step forward, each moment of progress is valuable and should be acknowledged. Remember, you are not alone in this journey; God is walking beside you, guiding and supporting you every step of the way. Embrace the path you're on and cherish each moment of growth.

Integrating self-care practices and spiritual disciplines isn't just about adding more tasks to your busy life; it's about putting your well-being first and acknowledging that you are a cherished child of God, worthy of love and care. Remember that true healing is a comprehensive journey that nourishes your body, mind, and spirit. It's about discovering yourself, nurturing compassion for yourself, and building a deep connection with your Creator. Embrace this journey with faith, hope, and the strong belief that restoration and wholeness are within your grasp. While the path might have its challenges, the destination—a life brimming with peace, joy, and freedom in Christ—is truly worth every step. Remember that your healing reflects God's incredible love and grace, shining a light on His transformative power in your life.

The journey to healing from past trauma is a multifaceted process, and a crucial element lies in rediscovering your true identity – the identity God intended for you, separate from the wounds and distortions inflicted by past hurts. This isn't about ignoring the pain but understanding that those experiences don't define your worth. Your identity is rooted in your relationship with God, and He sees you not as the sum of your traumas, but as His beloved child, created in His image, with unique gifts and purposes.

This rediscovery begins with actively rejecting the lies that trauma whispers. Trauma often distorts our self-perception, leading us to believe negative and untrue things about ourselves. We internalize the hurtful words and actions of others, accepting them as truths about our inherent worth. These are lies from the enemy, designed to steal your joy, your confidence, and your very sense of self. The Bible is replete with verses that directly challenge these lies and affirm your true identity in Christ.

Consider this: 2 Corinthians 5:17 states, "Therefore, if anyone is in Christ, the new creation has come: The old has gone, the new is here!" This verse speaks powerfully to God's transformative work in our lives. The old identity, shaped by trauma and negativity, is no longer who you are. You have been made new in Christ, cleansed and renewed by His grace. This new identity is not earned; it's a gift, freely given through faith in Jesus.

Romans 8:1 further emphasizes this truth: "Therefore, there is now no condemnation for those who are in Christ Jesus." The weight of past mistakes, the shame of past experiences, the guilt that relentlessly pursues you – these are all lifted when you embrace your identity in Christ. Condemnation is the weapon of the enemy, and it loses its power when we stand firmly on the truth of God's unconditional love and forgiveness.

Understanding this profound truth is the first step. But how do you actively embrace this new identity? It's a journey, not a destination, but here are some practical steps to help you navigate it:

Affirmations: Speak truth over yourself daily. Write down verses like Psalm 139:14 ("I praise you because I am fearfully and wonderfully made; your works are wonderful, I know that full well"), and speak them aloud, believing them in your heart. Create your own affirmations that reflect your new identity in Christ. For example, "I am loved unconditionally by God," or "I am strong, capable, and worthy of love." Repeat these affirmations throughout your day, especially when feelings of self-doubt arise.

Journaling: Continue your journaling practice, but shift the focus. Instead of simply venting or recounting past traumas, use your journal to document the ways God is working in your life. Record instances where you felt His love, His strength, His presence. Write about the positive attributes you see in yourself, recognizing the gifts and talents God has given you. Journaling becomes a tool for cultivating gratitude and self-awareness.

Prayer: This continues to be vital. Pray not only for healing but also for revelation of your true self. Ask God to show you your strengths, your passions, and your unique purpose in His kingdom. Ask Him to replace the negative self-talk with His voice of truth and love. Pray for His guidance in every area of your life, trusting in His wisdom and His perfect plan for you.

Forgiveness: Forgiveness is not for the other person; it's for you. Holding onto bitterness and resentment only perpetuates the pain and prevents you from moving forward. Forgiveness doesn't mean condoning what happened; it means releasing the grip those experiences have on your heart and mind. This process takes time and may require professional help, but it is essential for claiming your new identity. Consider journaling about the people you need to forgive. Write down how their actions impacted you, and write a letter (you don't have to send it) expressing your feelings. Then, pray for them and for yourself as you let go.

Identify Your Gifts: God has uniquely gifted each of us. Your past may have caused you to neglect or suppress these gifts, but they are still within you. Take time to reflect on your strengths and talents. What do you enjoy doing? What are you naturally good at? How can you use those gifts to serve God and others? This process will help you discover a sense of purpose and fulfillment, solidifying your identity in your role as a part of God's bigger picture.

Celebrate Your Victories: Healing is a process. There will be good days and bad days. Acknowledge and celebrate every victory, no matter how small. Did you resist the urge to engage in self-destructive behavior? Did you forgive someone? Did you speak a positive affirmation when you felt overwhelmed? These are all significant accomplishments on your journey toward wholeness. Keep a record of these moments to remind yourself of how far you've come.

Seek Community: Surround yourself with supportive people who believe in you and uplift you. This could be a small group at church, a support group, or simply close friends and family who understand your journey. Their encouragement and prayers are invaluable. This community serves as a constant reminder of your worth and belonging. Sharing your story with trusted friends or family can also provide further relief and healing.

Spiritual Disciplines: Continue practicing the spiritual disciplines mentioned earlier: meditation, prayer, journaling, and physical activity. These practices nourish your soul, strengthen your resilience, and help you connect with God's love and guidance. Each one serves as a tool for strengthening your inner being and reinforcing your newfound sense of self.

Rediscovering your identity in Christ is not a quick fix, but a transformative process that takes time, effort, and unwavering faith. It requires consistent effort, consistent self-compassion, and the unwavering belief that God is walking with you every step of the way. Embrace the journey with courage, knowing that God's love is your anchor and His truth is your foundation. He sees your worth, your beauty, and your potential, even when you can't see it yourself. Trust in His plan, and allow His love to shape your identity into something magnificent, surpassing your wildest dreams. Embrace the beautiful, empowered woman of valor God created you to be.

Chapter 4

Building Healthy Relationships

Building upon the foundation of rediscovering your identity in Christ, we now turn to the vital area of building healthy relationships. Understanding what constitutes a healthy relationship is crucial for breaking free from toxic patterns and creating a future filled with love, respect, and mutual support. God designed us for connection, for community, for the rich tapestry of relationships that enrich our lives and reflect His own loving nature. However, recognizing what constitutes a healthy relationship dynamic is essential to navigating this crucial area of life successfully and avoiding repeating past mistakes.

A vibrant interplay of several key elements characterizes healthy relationships. First and foremost is **open and honest communication**. This isn't simply about talking; it's about truly listening, understanding, and empathizing with your partner's perspective. It involves expressing your own needs and feelings clearly and respectfully, even when it's difficult. In a healthy relationship, both partners feel comfortable sharing their thoughts and emotions without fear of judgment or criticism. They actively seek to understand each other's viewpoints, even when they disagree. This involves actively listening to understand, not to respond, a skill that requires patience and a genuine desire to connect on a deeper level. Avoid interrupting, and practice reflective listening by summarizing what you've heard to ensure understanding.

Consider the example of a couple facing a financial challenge. In a healthy relationship, they'd openly discuss their concerns, collaboratively brainstorming solutions instead of resorting to blame or accusations. They'd listen to each other's anxieties, offering reassurance and support rather than dismissing their worries. This requires vulnerability, a willingness to expose one's weaknesses and insecurities, trusting that the other person will respond with compassion and understanding. This vulnerability is a testament to the strength of the bond, a willingness to lay bare one's heart and soul.

Another cornerstone of healthy relationships is **mutual respect**. This involves valuing your partner's opinions, beliefs, and feelings, even when they differ from your own. Respect is shown through words and actions, demonstrating consideration and kindness. It means avoiding belittling remarks, condescension, or controlling behaviors. A hallmark of disrespect is the erosion of the other person's boundaries, personal space, or autonomy. Healthy relationships recognize and respect individual boundaries, ensuring that each person feels safe and valued. This extends to respecting each other's time, personal space, and individual pursuits. It is about celebrating each other's uniqueness and supporting individual growth and aspirations.

Think about a scenario where one partner wants to pursue further education. In a healthy relationship, the other partner would support this ambition, even if it means temporary sacrifices or adjustments.

They would acknowledge the importance of personal growth and encourage their partner's pursuit of their goals. This support doesn't need to be unconditional, and reasonable expectations and healthy discussions around commitment and expectations are perfectly acceptable; the essential element is the underlying respect and desire for each other's well-being.

Closely intertwined with respect is **trust**. Trust is built over time through consistent honesty, reliability, and keeping commitments. It's the confidence that your partner has your best interests at heart and will act with integrity. This isn't a blind faith; it is built on a foundation of demonstrated reliability and consistent actions. In healthy relationships, there's a shared understanding of expectations, and transparency is paramount. This is particularly vital when navigating conflict, which is inevitable in any relationship. Trust means believing that disagreements can be resolved through constructive communication and mutual compromise rather than destructive power struggles.

Imagine a situation where one partner is late for an important event. In a healthy relationship, characterized by trust, there would be an open explanation without suspicion or accusations. The trust facilitates a discussion about the reason for the lateness, and any potential anxieties are addressed with empathy and understanding. Conversely, a relationship lacking trust might interpret the lateness as a deliberate act of disregard, escalating into unnecessary conflict.

Mutual support is another crucial component. This means providing encouragement, assistance, and emotional support during both good times and bad. A healthy relationship is a haven of support where both partners feel encouraged to pursue their dreams, overcome challenges, and celebrate their achievements. This involves being a sounding board, offering practical help, and providing a safe space for emotional expression. It means actively celebrating each other's triumphs and providing comfort and understanding during difficult times. This mutual support network isn't just emotional; it also extends to practical matters, offering assistance with daily tasks, responsibilities, and challenges.

Consider a couple facing a health crisis. In a healthy relationship, they offer each other unwavering support, both emotional and practical. They navigate the situation together, sharing responsibilities and offering encouragement. This mutual support allows them to face adversity together, strengthening their bond and deepening their commitment.

Beyond these core elements, several other indicators point toward healthy relationship dynamics. **Shared values and goals** provide a common foundation, aligning your life paths and providing direction. While not every aspect of life needs to be perfectly aligned, sharing fundamental values and long-term aspirations creates a sense of shared purpose and unity. **Emotional intimacy**—the ability to share vulnerable emotions and feelings—builds a profound connection, facilitating deeper understanding and empathy. This requires courage and vulnerability, creating a space where emotions can be shared safely and without fear of judgment.

Conflict resolution skills are essential. Disagreements are inevitable; how you handle them defines the health of the relationship. Healthy relationships prioritize respectful communication, finding constructive solutions, and avoiding manipulative or aggressive tactics. This is a crucial area that often needs focused attention and may even benefit from professional help. Learning effective conflict resolution strategies is crucial for building a strong and resilient relationship that can weather any storm.

Recognizing Unhealthy Patterns

Recognizing unhealthy patterns is equally important. Unhealthy relationships often involve control, manipulation, disrespect, and a lack of communication. Constant criticism, belittling, and emotional abuse are clear signs of toxicity. A lack of trust, characterized by suspicion, jealousy, and controlling behaviors, signals a troubled dynamic. These are subtle yet powerful indicators that demand careful consideration. Unhealthy relationships often involve an imbalance of power, where one partner consistently dominates or controls the other, leaving little space for personal autonomy or freedom of expression.

Understanding these indicators of both healthy and unhealthy relationships empowers you to make informed choices about your relationships. It allows you to set boundaries, protect yourself from harm, and cultivate relationships that nurture your spiritual, emotional, and mental well-being. It's a journey that requires discernment, courage, and a commitment to prioritizing your well-being. Remember that God designed you for healthy, fulfilling relationships. He wants you to experience the joy and blessing of mutual love and support. By understanding these healthy relationship dynamics, you can actively create relationships that honor God and reflect the beautiful tapestry of His creation. The journey toward healthy relationships is an ongoing process, requiring consistent effort and the willingness to learn and grow.

Choosing the right relationships is a crucial step in building a life that reflects God's design for our well-being. It's a journey of discernment, guided by biblical principles and a deep understanding of your own identity in Christ. While we've explored the characteristics of healthy relationships, the focus now shifts to the proactive selection of those relationships. This is not about judging others but about safeguarding your own spiritual, emotional, and mental health. God calls us to love our neighbors, but this love doesn't necessitate enduring unhealthy or toxic relationships.

The first step in choosing healthy relationships is self-awareness. Before seeking connection with others, take time to understand your own needs, values, and boundaries. Reflect on past relationships, identifying patterns of behavior and the roles you played. Were you drawn to people who controlled you, disrespected you, or consistently let you down? Understanding these patterns is key to avoiding them in future relationships. This self-reflection allows you to identify your weaknesses and areas that need healing, which allows you to seek support and then, with strength, build healthy relationships. Journaling, prayer, and possibly counseling can be invaluable tools in this process. Pray for guidance from God to reveal areas of your heart that may attract unhealthy relationships.

The Bible offers profound wisdom regarding the selection of companions. Proverbs 13:20 states, "Walk with the wise and become wise, for a companion of fools suffers harm." This verse highlights the importance of surrounding yourself with individuals who share your values and encourage your growth in Christ. This verse also provides a powerful image: walking in the path of life alongside others. Who are you walking with? Are they leading you closer to or further away from God? It's a powerful image to use to self-reflect. Look for individuals who embody Christ-like qualities: kindness, compassion, humility, integrity, and a genuine love for God and others. Seek those who uplift you spiritually, encourage your faith, and support your journey of becoming more like Christ. Avoid those who consistently pull you away from God or tempt you to compromise your values. Discernment is crucial; prayerfully seek guidance as you assess the character and intentions of those you are considering forming closer bonds with.

Recognizing red flags is another critical element in choosing healthy relationships. Red flags are warning signs that indicate potential toxicity or incompatibility. These signs aren't always blatant; they can be subtle behaviors or patterns that emerge over time. Learn to recognize these subtle yet critical warning signs. These warning signs could be dismissing your feelings, controlling behaviors, persistent negativity, or a lack of respect for your boundaries. It's important to trust your intuition. If something feels off or uncomfortable, don't ignore it. Your gut feeling is often an indicator of a potential problem. Don't minimize or dismiss these warning signs, thinking you can change the person. The Bible warns against unequal yokes (2 Corinthians 6:14), emphasizing the importance of finding partners who share your faith and values. If someone consistently displays behavior that contradicts your values or belief systems, it is a serious warning sign to take notice of.

Examples of red flags include attempts to isolate you from friends and family, consistent criticism or belittling, controlling behavior regarding your finances, social life, or personal choices, a history of abusive relationships, and unwillingness to compromise or communicate openly and honestly. Jealousy, possessiveness, and an inability to respect your personal boundaries should also be taken seriously. If you notice these patterns, don't ignore them; prioritize your well-being and safety. If you feel constantly anxious, afraid, or manipulated in a relationship, these are important warning signs that indicate a toxic and potentially harmful situation.

Choosing the right relationships involves setting healthy boundaries. Boundaries are the limits you set to protect your emotional, physical, and spiritual well-being. They are not about being selfish or unloving; they are about respecting yourself and your needs. This is a crucial aspect that many struggle with. Healthy boundaries protect us from being taken advantage of or manipulated, and they show others how we expect to be treated.

They clarify what behavior is acceptable and unacceptable within a relationship, ensuring mutual respect and a healthy power dynamic. God calls us to love others, but this love doesn't mean neglecting our own well-being or tolerating abuse. Boundaries are an act of self-love, ensuring that you are not taken advantage of.

Communicating your boundaries clearly and respectfully is essential. This might involve saying no to requests that make you feel uncomfortable or violated, or establishing clear expectations about communication styles and time commitments. It also means protecting your personal space and time. It may be difficult initially to assert your boundaries, especially if you are not used to doing so. God provides guidance and strength to set these boundaries. You may feel fear, guilt, or shame in setting boundaries, especially if you have a history of codependency or toxic relationships. Pray for strength and courage. Remember God empowers you to set these boundaries and honor yourself.

Once you've established healthy boundaries, consistently enforce them. This demonstrates respect for yourself and shows others that you are serious about protecting your well-being. Be prepared for resistance; some people may not understand or respect your boundaries. Don't give in to pressure; stand firm in your convictions. This may lead to conflict, but it's important to remember that setting and maintaining boundaries is an act of self-love and self-preservation.

Choosing the right relationships also involves being discerning in friendships. Surround yourself with people who encourage your growth in faith and support your journey toward wholeness. These friendships offer a safe space to share your struggles, celebrate your victories, and receive godly counsel. It's a place where accountability and mutual support are evident. Proverbs 27:17 states, "As iron sharpens iron, so one person sharpens another."

Choose friends who help you grow spiritually and challenge you to live a life pleasing to God. Avoid friendships that are based on gossip, negativity, or unhealthy competition.

In romantic relationships, choose someone who shares your faith and values, respects your boundaries, and supports your spiritual growth. This is crucial to building a relationship that honors God and endures. Seek someone who is emotionally mature, demonstrates integrity, and is committed to working through challenges in a healthy way. Avoid relationships built on infatuation, superficiality, or codependency. These relationships, while potentially exciting in the beginning, are often built on a shaky foundation. It's essential to take your time, prayerfully seek guidance, and ensure that your partner shares your commitment to a relationship built on mutual love and respect.

Finally, remember that choosing the right relationships is an ongoing process. As you grow and change, your needs and values may evolve, requiring adjustments in your relationships. Some relationships may end, while others may deepen and transform. Be open to change, and trust that God will guide you in making choices that reflect His will for your life. Continue to assess your relationships, identifying areas of strength and areas that need attention. Prayerfully seek God's guidance and wisdom, and remain open to making necessary changes that reflect His perfect will for your life. This continuous discernment is key to establishing and maintaining a life characterized by healthy and fulfilling relationships that honor God and bring you joy.

Effective Communication

Effective communication is the cornerstone of any healthy relationship, whether familial, platonic, or romantic. It's the bridge that connects hearts, fosters understanding, and resolves conflicts. In the context of Christian relationships, communication is not merely the exchange of information; it's a reflection of our love for God and our neighbors. It's an opportunity to embody Christ's teachings of compassion, empathy, and grace. Without effective communication, even the most well-intentioned relationships can crumble under the weight of misunderstanding and unresolved conflict.

The first step toward healthy communication is cultivating active listening. This means more than simply hearing the words someone speaks; it involves paying attention to their tone of voice, body language, and unspoken emotions. It requires a sincere desire to understand their perspective, even if you don't agree with it. Proverbs 18:13 reminds us, "To answer before listening—that is folly and shame." Before formulating a response, take the time to truly grasp the message being conveyed. This act of attentive listening shows respect, validation, and a genuine care for the other person. It demonstrates that their thoughts and feelings matter to you, a crucial element in building trust and intimacy.

Active listening involves asking clarifying questions to ensure complete understanding. Instead of interrupting or formulating your response while the other person is speaking, focus on their words and then ask questions to clarify any ambiguities. For instance, instead of jumping in with your own perspective, you might ask, "Can you tell me more about that?" or "What was it about that situation that made you feel that way?" This approach demonstrates a genuine desire to understand their experience and reduces the likelihood of misinterpretations and misunderstandings. This attentiveness also creates a safe space where the other person feels comfortable sharing their deepest thoughts and concerns without fear of judgment.

Beyond active listening, clear and honest self-expression is paramount. This involves articulating your needs, feelings, and boundaries in a respectful and assertive manner. It's crucial to avoid accusatory language or blaming others for your feelings. Instead of saying, "You always make me feel angry," try, "When I experience X, I feel Y because of Z." This approach focuses on your own experience, avoiding generalizations and personal attacks. It shifts the focus from blame to understanding, creating a more conducive environment for productive dialogue. Using "I" statements empowers you to take ownership of your emotions and reactions without placing blame on the other person. This approach not only promotes healthier communication but also cultivates empathy and mutual respect.

For example, if you feel overwhelmed by a friend's constant requests for help, instead of saying, "You always ask me for favors and it's too much," you could say, "I've been feeling overwhelmed lately, and I need some time to focus on my own responsibilities. I'd love to help when I'm better able to." This approach is honest, respectful, and clearly sets a boundary without alienating your friend. Remember, setting boundaries is not selfish; it is an act of self-preservation and respect for your own well-being. It demonstrates self-love and a commitment to your spiritual and emotional health.

When expressing needs, concerns, or boundaries, be mindful of your tone of voice and body language. Even the most well-intentioned words can be misinterpreted if accompanied by anger, sarcasm, or defensiveness. Maintain a calm and respectful demeanor, ensuring your nonverbal cues align with your verbal message. Remember, communication is not only about what you say but also how you say it. Your body language, tone of voice, and facial expressions often speak louder than words. By maintaining a calm demeanor, you create a safer space for open and honest communication, fostering trust and reducing defensiveness.

Healthy communication also involves practicing empathy. Empathy is the ability to understand and share the feelings of another person. It's about putting yourself in their shoes and seeing the world from their perspective. This doesn't mean you necessarily agree with their viewpoint, but it does require you to acknowledge and validate their feelings. 1 Corinthians 13:4-7 beautifully describes love, and a key component of love is empathy: "Love is patient, love is kind. It does not envy, it does not boast, it is not proud. It does not dishonor others, it is not self-seeking, it is not easily angered, it keeps no record of wrongs. Love does not delight in evil but rejoices with the truth. It always protects, always trusts, always hopes, always perseveres." Putting these principles into practice enhances your ability to communicate effectively.

Conflict is inevitable in any relationship, but the way we handle disagreements significantly impacts the health and longevity of the relationship. Instead of avoiding conflict or resorting to anger or accusations, aim for constructive conflict resolution. This involves approaching disagreements with a spirit of humility, seeking to understand the other person's perspective before presenting your own. Philippians 2:3-4 urges us to "Do nothing out of selfish ambition or vain conceit. Rather, in humility value others above yourselves, not looking to your own interests but each of you to the interests of the others." This approach is vital in navigating conflicts and building strong relationships.

During disagreements, focus on the issue at hand rather than launching personal attacks. Avoid name-calling, insults, or any form of verbal abuse. Remember that the goal is to resolve the conflict, not to win an argument. Instead of escalating the situation, strive to de-escalate it by remaining calm, listening actively, and expressing your concerns respectfully. This approach promotes mutual understanding and respect, fostering a healthy atmosphere for resolution. Remember that conflict is an opportunity for growth and deeper understanding; approaching it with a spirit of humility can strengthen your relationships.

If necessary, seek help from a neutral third party, such as a pastor, counselor, or trusted mentor. Sometimes, an outside perspective can help shed light on the situation and facilitate a more productive resolution. This outside perspective can offer guidance and support, aiding in the process of understanding and reconciliation. External help doesn't signify failure; instead it demonstrates a commitment to resolving conflict healthily and prioritizing the well-being of the relationship.

Finally, practice forgiveness. Holding onto resentment or anger will only poison the relationship. Forgiveness is not about condoning hurtful behavior; it's about releasing the burden of bitterness and choosing to move forward. Ephesians 4:32 encourages us to "Be kind and compassionate to one another, forgiving each other, just as in Christ forgave you." Forgiveness is a powerful tool in fostering healing and reconciliation. It not only benefits the other person but also frees you from the negativity and emotional weight of unforgiveness.

In conclusion, effective communication is a skill that requires consistent effort and practice. It is a journey, not a destination, and it involves cultivating active listening, clear self-expression, empathy, constructive conflict resolution, and forgiveness. By prioritizing these principles, you can build healthy relationships that honor God and reflect the love of Christ. Remember, the strength of your relationships depends on the quality of your communication. Invest time and effort in mastering this crucial skill, and you will reap the blessings of strong, fulfilling, and God-honoring connections.

Forgiveness is Not Weakness

Forgiveness isn't a sign of weakness; it's a testament to strength. It's a conscious decision to release the bitterness and resentment that can fester within us, poisoning not only our relationships but also our own hearts. In the Christian context, forgiveness is not merely a suggestion; it's a command rooted in the very essence of our faith. Jesus' teachings on forgiveness are pervasive, emphasizing its importance in our journey toward spiritual maturity and healthy relationships. The parable of the unforgiving servant in Matthew 18:23-35 serves as a powerful reminder of the consequences of withholding forgiveness, both for ourselves and those we hold accountable. The Father's boundless mercy shown to us should inspire us to extend the same grace to others.

The process of forgiveness is rarely easy. It requires a willingness to confront painful emotions, acknowledge the hurt inflicted, and consciously choose to release the burden of resentment. It's not about condoning the actions of another; rather, it's about freeing ourselves from the chains of bitterness that bind us to the past. The journey toward forgiveness is deeply personal, and the timeline varies from person to person. Some wounds heal quickly, while others require significant time and effort. It's important to be patient with yourself and allow the healing process to unfold naturally, seeking guidance and support from trusted friends, family, mentors, or spiritual advisors as needed.

One of the initial hurdles in practicing forgiveness is often self-forgiveness. We are all imperfect beings, prone to making mistakes and causing hurt to others, unintentionally or otherwise. Holding onto guilt and self-recrimination can be just as damaging as holding onto resentment toward others. Self-forgiveness requires acknowledging our failings, accepting responsibility for our actions, and extending the same grace to ourselves that we extend to others. This involves recognizing that our mistakes do not define us and that God's love and forgiveness are unconditional. Remember 1 John 1:9, "If we confess our sins, he is faithful and just and will forgive us our sins and purify us from all unrighteousness." This verse offers a profound assurance of God's willingness to forgive us, enabling us to extend that same forgiveness to ourselves.

Forgiving others, particularly those who have caused us significant pain, requires a significant commitment. It may involve confronting the person who hurt us, expressing our feelings, and seeking reconciliation. However, forgiveness doesn't necessitate reconciliation; forgiveness is primarily an internal process of releasing the resentment and bitterness that hinder our own well-being. In some situations, reconciliation may not be possible or safe, especially in cases of abuse or betrayal where the other person is unwilling to take responsibility or change their behavior. In such instances, forgiveness does not mean we need to maintain a relationship with the person who hurt us. It simply means releasing ourselves from the emotional burden of unforgiveness and allowing ourselves to heal.

A helpful approach to forgiving others is to actively practice empathy. Try to understand the other person's perspective, even if you don't agree with their actions. Consider their background, their life experiences, and the factors that might have contributed to their behavior. This doesn't excuse their actions but can help us to gain a deeper understanding and potentially release some of the anger and resentment we may be holding. Remember, empathy is not about condoning harmful behavior; it's about attempting to understand the human complexities that underlie it.

Forgiveness is an ongoing process, not a one-time event. There may be times when old wounds resurface, requiring renewed effort and commitment to forgive. This is natural and expected; it does not signify a failure in forgiveness, but rather an indication of the depth and complexity of the healing process. It's important to be patient and persistent in our efforts, remembering that true forgiveness is a gradual process of letting go.

Beyond interpersonal relationships, forgiveness is crucial in our relationship with God. We all fall short of God's perfect standard, and acknowledging our failings and seeking his forgiveness is essential for spiritual growth. Recognizing our dependence on God's grace allows us to extend that same grace to others. The act of confessing our sins and seeking forgiveness from God creates a space for healing and restoration in our spiritual lives. This reconciliation allows us to approach our relationships with a renewed sense of humility and compassion.

Building healthy relationships requires not just forgiveness but also the ability to address conflicts constructively. Disagreements are inevitable in any relationship, but it's how we handle those disagreements that determines the health and longevity of the relationship. Instead of avoiding conflict or resorting to anger and accusations, we should strive to engage in constructive conflict resolution. This involves approaching disagreements with humility, listening attentively to the other person's perspective, and expressing our own feelings and needs clearly and respectfully.

Active Listening

Active listening plays a vital role in constructive conflict resolution. It's not just about hearing the words someone speaks but also about understanding the underlying emotions and concerns. Asking clarifying questions, reflecting back what we heard, and validating the other person's feelings all contribute to creating a safe space for open and honest communication. This is especially critical during disagreements where strong emotions might be involved.

Another important element of constructive conflict resolution is assertive communication. This involves expressing our needs and boundaries clearly and respectfully, without being aggressive or passive-aggressive. Using "I" statements helps to focus on our own feelings and experiences without blaming or accusing the other person. For example, instead of saying "You always make me angry," we can say "I feel angry when...." This subtle shift in language can significantly change the tone of the conversation and reduce defensiveness.

Setting boundaries is also essential for healthy relationships. Boundaries protect our physical, emotional, and spiritual well-being. They are not a sign of selfishness but rather a way of respecting ourselves and our needs. Clearly communicating our boundaries to others helps to prevent misunderstandings and conflicts and ensures that our needs are respected. This can involve setting limits on time, energy, or emotional investment.

When disagreements arise, it's crucial to focus on the issue at hand rather than launching personal attacks. Avoiding name-calling, insults, or any form of verbal abuse is paramount. Remember that the goal is to resolve the conflict, not to win an argument. Taking time to cool down before engaging in a difficult conversation can also help ensure that the communication remains productive and respectful.

If constructive dialogue doesn't lead to a resolution, seeking help from a neutral third party, such as a counselor or trusted mentor, can be beneficial. A mediator can help facilitate communication, offer unbiased insights, and guide the parties involved toward a mutually acceptable resolution. This doesn't indicate failure; instead, it demonstrates a commitment to resolving conflict healthily and prioritizing the well-being of the relationship.

Finally, practicing forgiveness is essential for maintaining healthy relationships. Holding onto resentment or anger poisons the relationship and hinders healing. Forgiveness doesn't mean condoning hurtful behavior; it means releasing the burden of bitterness and choosing to move forward. It's a crucial part of the reconciliation process, allowing us to restore trust and rebuild the relationship.

In conclusion, building and maintaining healthy relationships requires a commitment to effective communication, constructive conflict resolution, and forgiveness. These principles, when combined with a foundation of faith and reliance on God's grace, allow us to experience the fullness of life and the joy of meaningful connections. Through consistent effort and the application of biblical principles, we can cultivate relationships that honor God and reflect his love in the world. Remember, healthy relationships are not a destination but a journey that requires continual growth, effort, and a willingness to extend grace and forgiveness to both ourselves and others. The rewards of this journey, however, are immeasurable.

Adapting to Change

Maintaining healthy relationships isn't a one-time achievement; it's an ongoing process requiring consistent effort, intentional choices, and a commitment to growth. Just as a gardener diligently tends to their plants, nurturing them with water, sunlight, and care, so too must we nurture our relationships to ensure they thrive. This involves proactively addressing challenges, maintaining open communication, and adapting to the ever-changing dynamics of life.

One crucial aspect of maintaining healthy relationships is the ability to adapt to change. Life inevitably throws curveballs – job changes, moves, the birth of children, financial difficulties, or health challenges – all of which can impact our relationships. These transitions can strain even the strongest bonds, requiring flexibility, understanding, and a willingness to adapt our communication styles and expectations. Openly discussing these changes and how they affect each other is paramount. This requires vulnerability and a willingness to express anxieties and concerns without judgment. Focusing on mutual support and understanding during these periods strengthens the foundation of the relationship.

Communication remains the cornerstone of any healthy relationship. However, maintaining open and honest communication requires consistent effort and intentionality. It's not enough to simply talk; we must strive for *active* listening, where we truly hear and understand our partner's perspective, even if we don't agree with it. This involves setting aside distractions, making eye contact, and asking clarifying questions to ensure complete understanding. Furthermore, we must articulate our own thoughts and feelings clearly and respectfully, avoiding accusatory language or blaming. Using "I" statements, such as "I feel hurt when..." instead of "You always...", can significantly improve communication by reducing defensiveness and promoting empathy.

Regular quality time is crucial for maintaining intimacy and connection. In our busy lives, it's easy to let relationships fall by the wayside, neglecting the essential need for shared experiences and emotional connection. Scheduling dedicated time for each other, free from distractions, is a powerful way to nurture the relationship. This doesn't have to be extravagant; a simple walk together, a shared meal, or a quiet evening conversation can foster intimacy and strengthen the bond. The key is to focus on presence and connection rather than merely coexisting.

Another critical element is demonstrating appreciation and affection. Small acts of kindness, words of affirmation, and thoughtful gestures go a long way in showing love and appreciation. These expressions of love nurture the relationship and remind each other of their value and importance. Expressing gratitude for both big and small things strengthens the emotional bond and reinforces positive feelings. Regular acts of service, such as helping with chores or running errands, also demonstrate love and care. Remember the words of 1 Corinthians 13:4-7: "Love is patient, love is kind. It does not envy, it does not boast, it is not proud. It does not dishonor others, it is not self-seeking, it is not easily angered, it keeps no record of wrongs. Love does not delight in evil but rejoices with the truth. It always protects, always trusts, always hopes, always perseveres." This passage serves as a powerful guide for nurturing healthy relationships.

Conflict is inevitable in any relationship, but how we handle disagreements determines the strength of the bond. We must learn to navigate disagreements constructively instead of avoiding conflicts or engaging in destructive arguments. This involves approaching conflicts with a spirit of humility, recognizing that both parties may have valid points. Compromise and mutual understanding are essential to resolving conflicts healthily. Focusing on solutions rather than assigning blame allows for a more productive resolution.

Setting healthy boundaries is essential for maintaining self-respect and preserving the integrity of the relationship. Boundaries are not walls designed to shut others out; rather, they are guidelines designed to protect our physical, emotional, and spiritual well-being. Clearly communicating our boundaries and respecting the boundaries of others establishes a foundation of mutual respect. This might involve setting limits on time commitments, emotional investment, or even physical touch. Boundaries allow for healthy independence while maintaining a strong connection.

Regular reflection and evaluation of the relationship's health are also important. Periodically taking time to assess the state of the relationship and discussing areas of strength and areas needing improvement is vital for continued growth. Openly discussing concerns and addressing potential issues before they escalate prevents resentment and fosters ongoing progress. This involves honest self-reflection and a willingness to acknowledge our own contributions to any challenges the relationship faces.

Seeking external support when needed is a sign of strength, not weakness. Sometimes, seeking guidance from a trusted mentor, counselor, or pastor can provide invaluable support and perspective. An objective third party can offer fresh insights, guide communication, and help navigate difficult issues. This doesn't signify failure; rather, it shows a commitment to resolving challenges and prioritizing the health of the relationship. Remember, God provides community and support systems to aid us on our journey.

Forgiveness remains a crucial element in maintaining healthy relationships. Holding onto resentment or bitterness erodes trust and prevents healing. Even when it's difficult, forgiving others frees us from the burden of negativity and allows the relationship to move forward. Remember, forgiveness is not about condoning harmful behavior; it's about releasing the anger and bitterness that keep us bound to the past. It's a process, not a single act, requiring patience, grace, and a commitment to healing.

Cultivating a strong spiritual foundation within each individual strengthens the relationship itself. Shared faith can provide a common ground for values, morality, and purpose. Praying together, attending church services, or engaging in Bible study can deepen intimacy and enhance spiritual growth, strengthening the couple's bond. Shared spiritual practices offer comfort, guidance, and a framework for navigating life's challenges.

Finally, remember that maintaining healthy relationships is an ongoing journey, not a destination. It requires consistent effort, open communication, mutual respect, and a commitment to growth. By actively practicing these principles, rooted in faith and guided by God's love, we can cultivate relationships that are strong, fulfilling, and honoring to God. The rewards of these efforts are immeasurable, bringing joy, peace, and a deep sense of belonging. The journey may be challenging at times, but the destination – a thriving relationship built on a foundation of faith and love – is worth every step.

Chapter 5

Discovering God's Purpose for your Life

Understanding God's plan for your life is a journey of discovery, a pilgrimage of faith that unfolds over time. It's not a destination to be reached in a single leap, but rather a path to be walked, one step at a time, guided by the gentle hand of the Divine. This path is unique to each individual, a personalized tapestry woven with our gifts, talents, experiences, and the overarching narrative of God's love and grace. To embark on this journey is to embrace a lifelong quest for purpose, a quest that brings profound meaning and fulfillment.

The Bible is replete with examples of individuals who, through faith and obedience, discovered and fulfilled God's unique purpose for their lives. Consider Abraham, called by God to leave his homeland and journey to a promised land. Abraham's obedience, despite the uncertainties and challenges, led to the establishment of a nation through whom God's blessings would flow to the world. His journey was not without trials and tribulations, yet his unwavering faith ultimately resulted in a legacy that continues to resonate through millennia. His story is a powerful reminder that

God's plan may often lead us to places we would never choose for ourselves, yet these unexpected paths are often the most fruitful.

Similarly, consider Joseph, sold into slavery by his brothers, yet ultimately rising to become second in command in Egypt. His journey was marked by betrayal, imprisonment, and suffering, yet through these trials, God prepared him for a role that would save his family and an entire nation from famine. Joseph's story teaches us that God's hand is at work even in the darkest moments, shaping our lives and preparing us for our unique purposes. His story is a powerful testament to God's sovereignty and His ability to transform adversity into triumph. His life stands as a beacon of hope, illuminating the path for those who feel lost or betrayed, showing them that even in the depths of despair, God's plan is unfolding.

The prophet Jeremiah, initially hesitant and reluctant, was called by God to deliver difficult messages to the people of Judah. He faced opposition, persecution, and imprisonment, yet he persevered, fulfilling his prophetic calling with unwavering dedication. His life demonstrates the importance of obedience to God's calling, even when it's difficult or unpopular. Jeremiah's struggles, his doubts, and his eventual acceptance of his calling offer profound lessons in humility, perseverance, and trust in God's plan, even when it seems impossible. His story serves as a powerful reminder that our individual purposes may often require us to confront difficult truths and face opposition, but that in doing so, we fulfill God's will and contribute to His greater plan.

Initially a shepherd boy, David was anointed by God to be king of Israel. His journey was fraught with challenges, battles, and personal struggles, yet he remained faithful to God, ultimately becoming one of the greatest kings in Israel's history. David's life demonstrates the transformative power of God's grace and the potential for greatness that lies within each of us, no matter our humble beginnings. His life serves as an inspiration for those who feel inadequate or overlooked, reminding them that God sees our potential even when we cannot. He shows us that through faith and obedience, seemingly ordinary lives can become extraordinary instruments in God's hands.

These biblical examples highlight several key principles in understanding God's plan for your life. Firstly, it requires a willingness to listen to God's voice. This involves cultivating a relationship with God through prayer, Bible study, and seeking guidance from trusted mentors. It's a journey of attentiveness, of learning to discern God's whispers amidst the noise of the world. This often requires setting aside time for quiet reflection and prayer, creating space for God to speak. Active listening, a willingness to hear what God may be saying, is crucial to understanding His plan. This may involve seeking guidance from trusted mentors, pastors, or spiritual advisors.

Secondly, understanding God's plan often involves embracing uncertainty and stepping outside our comfort zones. God rarely reveals His plan in a grand, sweeping revelation; instead, He often guides us through a series of small steps, each revealing more of the overall picture. This necessitates faith and trust, a willingness to step out in obedience, even when the path ahead is unclear. This often requires surrender, letting go of our own plans and trusting in God's guidance, even when it feels risky.

Thirdly, discerning God's plan often requires perseverance through trials and challenges. The individuals mentioned above faced immense difficulties, yet they persevered, remaining faithful to God's calling. Our journeys are rarely easy; trials are inevitable, and they refine our faith and deepen our understanding of God's purposes for our lives.

Fourthly, God often uses our gifts, talents, and experiences to fulfill His purpose. Understanding your unique talents and passions is crucial to discerning how God may be calling you to serve. This involves self-reflection, prayerful consideration, and seeking feedback from trusted friends and family. Understanding your strengths and weaknesses provides insight into areas where God may be calling you to serve. It's about recognizing your abilities and how they align with God's purposes.

Finally, remember that God's plan is always for your good and His glory. Even when challenges arise, know that God is working all things together for your ultimate good (Romans 8:28). This understanding provides a powerful foundation for navigating life's uncertainties, bringing peace and assurance amidst challenges.

Discovering God's Purpose

Discovering God's purpose for your life is not a passive exercise but a dynamic, interactive journey. It requires active engagement, seeking guidance, and consistent steps of faith. It's about aligning your will with God's will, allowing Him to shape and mold you into the person He desires you to be. This journey will invariably involve moments of doubt, uncertainty, and even failure. But through it all, remember that God's love for you is unwavering, His plan is perfect, and His grace is sufficient. Embrace the journey, trust in His guidance, and rest assured that He will lead you to a life of purpose and fulfillment, a life that glorifies Him and blesses others. The path may be winding, the destination may not always be clear, but the journey itself is a testament to God's unwavering love and care for each of His children. As you seek to understand His plan, remember that His love is the compass that guides your way, and His grace is the strength that sustains you.

In moments of crisis and hardship, it's easy to feel lost and overwhelmed, consumed by the weight of trauma or the unexpected twists of life. Whether it comes in the form of loss, betrayal, or sudden change, trauma can shatter our sense of stability and safety. In these times, many individuals find themselves grappling with pain and uncertainty, searching for a way to navigate through their struggles. A powerful remedy exists amid this turmoil: trusting in God and His ability to help us overcome life's challenges.

The concept of trust, particularly trust in God, often seems simplistic, especially in the face of overwhelming pain. However, it's in this very simplicity that profound strength lies. Trusting in God's power means acknowledging that, although we may not understand the reasons for our suffering or the direction of our lives, there is a divine plan greater than our comprehension. This trust is not a denial of our feelings or experiences but an invitation to find peace amid chaos.

Many biblical figures faced substantial trauma and adversity. Consider the story of Job, who lost everything—his wealth, his health, and his family. Instead of surrendering to despair, Job clung to his faith in God. His journey through suffering is a testament to the transformative power of trusting in divine wisdom amidst life's unpredictability. Job's story teaches us that while pain is an inevitable part of life, our response to that pain can either lead us toward despair or closer to God.

When we face trauma or unexpected life surprises, we often grapple with feelings of isolation. It's important to remember that we are not alone in our struggles. God walks beside us during our darkest hours. Even when we feel abandoned or overwhelmed, God remains a steadfast presence. Psalm 23 beautifully expresses this sentiment: "Even though I walk through the darkest valley, I fear no evil, for you are with me." Recognizing that the divine accompanies us through our trials can provide immense comfort and strength.

Moreover, trusting in God's power allows us to redefine our understanding of trauma. Instead of viewing ourselves solely as victims, we can shift our perspective to see ourselves as survivors—individuals who have the strength to rise above their circumstances. This shift is crucial in the healing process and can empower us to seek not only recovery but also growth. As we trust God to guide us, we can begin to see our trauma not just as a source of pain but as a potential catalyst for personal transformation.

Surrounding ourselves with a supportive community can also be significant in our healing journey. When facing trauma, sharing our experiences with others can lighten the burden. Faith communities can provide a safe space for individuals to express their pain and find solace in shared beliefs. Individuals often come together to support one another through prayers, counseling, and fellowship. Being part of a faith-based community can remind us that we are not alone; together, we can lift each other up, reaffirm our trust in God, and navigate the complexities of life's challenges.

It's essential to acknowledge that healing is not a linear process. Trauma can resurface at unexpected times, triggering feelings that we thought we had overcome. However, trusting in God's power can give us the resilience to confront these emotions head-on. Rather than shying away from pain, we can invite it into our lives with the understanding that God is with us, providing the strength to endure. Philippians 4:13 reminds us that we can do all things through Christ who strengthens us. This scripture reassures us that even in moments of weakness, we can find empowerment through faith.

Practically, there are several ways to cultivate trust in God amidst trauma and life's surprises. Engaging in regular prayer can foster a deeper connection with the divine. It is a space where we can voice our fears, seek guidance, and ultimately find peace. Additionally, reading scripture can provide much-needed inspiration and perspective. The Bible is filled with promises of hope, resilience, and love that can nourish our spirits and reinforce our trust in God's plan.

Journaling is another helpful tool. Writing down our thoughts, prayers, and feelings can serve as an outlet for our emotional turmoil. This practice allows us to reflect on our journey, document our growth, and see how God has been present in our lives, even during difficult times. As we look back on our writings, we can witness the hand of God guiding us through moments of darkness and leading us to the light.

Always remember that life is unpredictable, often filled with trauma and surprises that can leave us feeling vulnerable. Yet, amid these trials, trusting in God's power can become our anchor. We can find resilience in our struggles by leaning into our faith, sharing our burdens with our communities, and embracing our journey. Through trust, we acknowledge not only our pain but also the profound strength that comes from believing in a higher purpose. No matter what we face, we are never truly alone—God is always by our side, ready to help us overcome and thrive in the face of adversity.

Understanding God's purpose for your life necessitates a deep understanding of yourself, specifically the gifts and talents He has bestowed upon you. These are not merely skills acquired through education or experience, but rather inherent abilities, divinely implanted, designed to be used in service to Him and others. Identifying these gifts is a crucial step in aligning your life with God's plan, unlocking your potential for significant impact, and experiencing the profound fulfillment that comes from living a purpose-driven life.

Discovering Your Spiritual Gifts

The Bible frequently speaks of spiritual gifts, highlighting their importance in building up the church and fulfilling God's mission in the world. 1 Corinthians 12:4-7, for example, lists a diverse array of gifts, including prophecy, teaching, serving, encouragement, giving, leading, and showing mercy. These are not simply talents; they are expressions of God working through believers, empowering them to serve effectively within the body of Christ. Recognizing your spiritual gifts is not about boasting or self-promotion; it's about humble discernment, seeking to understand how God has uniquely equipped you to contribute to His kingdom.

One effective method for identifying your spiritual gifts is through self-reflection and prayerful consideration. Take time to examine your life, reflecting on areas where you naturally excel, activities that bring you joy and a sense of fulfillment, and situations where you feel particularly energized and empowered. What comes easily to you? What do you enjoy doing, even when it requires effort? What activities leave you feeling drained and frustrated, and conversely, what activities leave you feeling refreshed and invigorated?

This process of introspection should be guided by prayer. Ask God to reveal your spiritual gifts to you. Seek His guidance in understanding your strengths and weaknesses, and how He might want to use you in His service. Consider journaling your thoughts and observations. Write down instances where you believe you've utilized a particular skill or talent effectively, and reflect on its positive impact. Pray over these instances, asking God for clarity on whether these are indeed gifts He has bestowed upon you.

It's crucial to remember that spiritual gifts are not static; they are often revealed and refined through experience and growth over time. What you might perceive as a minor talent today could blossom into a significant gift as you mature in your faith and deepen your relationship with God. Be patient with this process; it is a journey of discovery, not a race to arrive at an immediate conclusion.

Beyond self-reflection and prayer, seeking feedback from trusted individuals is immensely valuable. Share your observations and reflections with close friends, family members, mentors, or church leaders who know you well. Ask them to honestly assess your strengths and areas where they have seen you excel. Their perspective can provide valuable insights you may have overlooked in your own self-assessment. However, remember to discern their input prayerfully. While valuable, their observations should not be the sole determinant of your spiritual gifts; rather, they should serve as supplementary information to confirm or challenge your own insights.

Engaging in various ministry roles and activities within your church or community can also help you identify your gifts. Experiment with different areas of service, such as teaching Sunday School, leading a small group, serving in hospitality, or participating in outreach ministries. Observe how you feel in these different roles. Where do you feel most at home? Where do you thrive and find a sense of fulfillment? These experiences provide valuable opportunities for self-discovery and for God to reveal your inherent talents.

Remember that some spiritual gifts are more outwardly focused, while others are more inwardly oriented. Outwardly focused gifts involve direct service to others, such as teaching, preaching, evangelism, or leadership. Inwardly oriented gifts often support the work of those with more outward-facing gifts, such as prayer, intercession, encouragement, or giving. Understanding this diversity is vital; both types of gifts are crucial to the overall health and growth of the body of Christ. Do not undervalue the quiet, supportive roles; they are often essential to the functioning of the whole.

Identifying your spiritual gifts is not a one-time event, but rather an ongoing process of discernment and growth. As you mature in your faith, you may discover new gifts or find that existing gifts develop and expand in new and unexpected ways. Be open to this continuous process of revelation, allowing God to lead you into a deeper understanding of yourself and your role in God's kingdom. Embrace your unique talents with humility, using them to serve God and others, and experience the immeasurable joy of fulfilling the purpose He has prepared for you.

The process of discovering your gifts is intricately tied to your understanding of your character and personality. This understanding offers another layer to your self-reflection. Are you a highly organized individual with a meticulous attention to detail? This might suggest a gift for administration or planning within a ministry context. Are you a natural encourager, always ready with a kind word and a listening ear? Your gift may lie in nurturing and supporting others. Are you a persuasive communicator, easily able to articulate complex ideas in a way that is both engaging and accessible? This suggests a gift for teaching or preaching. Do you find yourself drawn to helping others solve their problems? A gift for counseling or reconciliation might be at play. These are simply examples; the possibilities are as diverse as God's people.

Consider your past experiences. Have you been consistently drawn to certain types of activities throughout your life? These inclinations could hint at underlying gifts waiting to be discovered. Think back to childhood passions, hobbies, or areas where you felt naturally inclined to excel. Were you always the one organizing games in the neighborhood? Did you consistently find yourself offering solace to your peers? Did you exhibit exceptional leadership qualities even in youth? These early indications can offer valuable insights into your potential gifts and talents.

It's important to recognize that identifying your spiritual gifts isn't simply about finding a niche within a church or ministry setting. It's about discovering how God desires to use your unique abilities in every aspect of your life – your family, your workplace, your community. Your gifts are not confined to the walls of a church building; they are designed to impact the world around you. This involves recognizing the intersections between your faith and your daily life, applying your spiritual gifts to your professional roles, your relationships, and your interactions with people from all walks of life. This broadened perspective allows for a fuller understanding of God's purpose for your life.

Remember, spiritual gifts are not earned or achieved; they are freely given by God. This truth releases the pressure of self-reliance and encourages dependence on Him. This is crucial because it shifts the focus from personal achievement to God's glory. The purpose of identifying your spiritual gifts is not to elevate yourself but to better understand how God wishes to use you to serve and bless others. This understanding helps eliminate pride and cultivates humility, essential qualities for effective service within His kingdom.

The Bible offers rich examples of individuals who utilized their spiritual gifts to make a profound impact. Consider Paul's missionary journeys, fueled by his gift of teaching and evangelism. Observe the quiet service of Dorcas, known for her acts of mercy and compassion. Remember the unwavering faith and prayers of those who were instrumental in the early church's growth. These examples demonstrate the remarkable diversity of gifts and their profound influence on the advancement of God's kingdom. Each gift, no matter how seemingly small, plays a vital role.

Finally, remember that understanding your spiritual gifts is a journey, not a destination. It's a process of continual discernment, guided by prayer and reflection, shaped by experience and the leading of God. Remain open to new revelations, be willing to adapt and grow, and trust in God's plan to use you in mighty ways. His purpose for your life is a beautiful and dynamic tapestry woven with your unique gifts and talents, designed to bring glory to Him and bless the world around you. The path toward discovering this purpose is an ongoing adventure of faith, a testament to His love and grace. Embrace this journey with humility, and allow Him to shape you into the person He intended you to be.

Overcoming Obstacles

The journey to discovering and fulfilling God's purpose is rarely a smooth, uninterrupted path. Obstacles and fears, often rooted in insecurity, doubt, or external pressures, frequently arise to impede our progress. These challenges are not necessarily signs of God's disapproval; rather, they are opportunities for growth, testing our faith and deepening our reliance on Him. Understanding and overcoming these hurdles is crucial for aligning our lives with His divine plan.

One common obstacle is the fear of failure. The thought of not measuring up, of falling short of expectations – both our own and others' – can be paralyzing. We may hesitate to step out of our comfort zones, fearing the potential for embarrassment or disappointment. This fear often stems from a misplaced focus on self-reliance rather than trusting in God's grace and strength. The Bible reminds us that we are not alone in this journey; God promises to equip us with everything we need to fulfill His purpose. Philippians 4:13 assures us, "I can do all this through him who gives me strength." This verse is not a promise of effortless success, but rather an affirmation of God's enabling power even in the face of adversity. Failure, in the context of faith, becomes an opportunity for learning and growth, refining our character and strengthening our dependence on God.

Doubt is another significant obstacle. Questioning God's plan, His timing, or even His existence, is a common experience, particularly during challenging times. These doubts are not necessarily indicators of a lack of faith; rather, they can be opportunities to deepen our understanding of God and to strengthen our relationship with Him. The book of Job powerfully illustrates the wrestling with doubt. Job's unwavering faith was tested through immense suffering, yet he ultimately reaffirmed his trust in God's sovereignty and goodness. The key is to approach our doubts with honesty and humility, bringing them before God in prayer, seeking wisdom and understanding. James 1:5-6 encourages us: "If any of you lacks wisdom, you should ask God, who gives generously to all without finding fault, and it will be given to you."

Insecurity can also hinder us from embracing God's purpose. Feelings of inadequacy, self-doubt, and a lack of self-worth can prevent us from taking risks or stepping into leadership roles. These feelings often stem from past experiences, unmet expectations, or negative self-talk. The antidote to insecurity is found in recognizing our identity in Christ. We are not defined by our failures or limitations, but by our relationship with God. Ephesians 2:10 declares, "For we are God's handiwork, created in Christ Jesus to do good works, which God prepared in advance for us to do." This verse reminds us that we are created for a purpose, and our worth is not determined by our accomplishments but by our inherent value as children of God.

External pressures from family, friends, or societal expectations can also significantly impact our pursuit of God's purpose. These pressures may involve criticism, disapproval, or even outright opposition. It is crucial to discern between constructive feedback and destructive criticism. Constructive criticism can help us to refine our approach and avoid pitfalls, while destructive criticism seeks to undermine our confidence and dissuade us from our calling. Learning to establish healthy boundaries is essential in navigating these pressures. We must be discerning in seeking advice and counsel, ensuring that it aligns with God's Word and our own conscience. Proverbs 3:5-6 advises us to "Trust in the Lord with all your heart and lean not on your own understanding; in all your ways submit to him, and he will make your paths straight."

Overcoming these obstacles requires intentional strategies rooted in faith. Prayer is paramount; it is the lifeline connecting us to God's strength, wisdom, and guidance. Through consistent, heartfelt prayer, we can receive encouragement, clarity, and the courage to face our fears and doubts. Scripture study provides a foundation of truth and encouragement, equipping us with the knowledge and promises of God to navigate challenging situations. Surrounding ourselves with a supportive community of faith is also vital. Fellow believers can offer prayer, encouragement, and accountability, providing a safe space to share struggles and celebrate victories. Seeking wise counsel from mentors or spiritual leaders provides an objective perspective and guidance rooted in biblical principles.

Consider the life of Moses. He initially resisted God's call, citing his inadequacy (Exodus 3:11-12). God, however, equipped him with the necessary abilities and empowered him through Aaron's assistance. Moses's journey demonstrates that God often uses those who feel unqualified, transforming their weaknesses into strengths through His grace. Similarly, David, a seemingly insignificant shepherd boy, rose to become king, demonstrating God's capacity to work through unlikely individuals. Even amidst battles and treachery, David relied on God's strength and guidance. His life stands as a powerful testament to God's ability to overcome adversity and equip individuals for remarkable achievements.

Furthermore, the Apostle Paul, initially a persecutor of Christians, underwent a dramatic transformation, becoming one of Christianity's most influential figures. His life serves as a powerful illustration of God's redemptive power and His capacity to use past failures for future glory. Paul's experiences highlight the transformative nature of God's grace and the possibility of overcoming even the deepest insecurities and past mistakes. His unwavering faith, despite persecution and hardship, became a beacon of hope and inspiration for generations.

Remember, the path to fulfilling God's purpose is a journey of faith, not a sprint. There will be moments of doubt, periods of uncertainty, and challenges that test our resilience. However, through consistent prayer, Scripture study, community support, and wise counsel, we can overcome obstacles and fears, embracing the incredible journey God has prepared for us. Embrace the process, trust in His unwavering love, and allow Him to shape you into the person He designed you to be, equipped to fulfill the unique and significant purpose He has for your life. Our fears or insecurities do not limit his plan; it is empowered by His grace and sustained by His strength. Trust in Him, and embark on this transformative journey with courage and unwavering faith. The reward of living a purpose-driven life, aligned with God's will, is immeasurable joy, profound fulfillment, and a legacy that extends far beyond our own lifetimes.

Seeking God's Guidance

Having established the potential roadblocks on the path to discovering God's purpose, let's now delve into the practical methods for seeking His guidance. This isn't a passive process; it requires active engagement with God and a willingness to listen to His voice. It's a journey of faith, requiring trust, humility, and perseverance. The destination—a life lived in alignment with God's will—is worth the effort.

Prayer forms the cornerstone of seeking God's guidance. It's not merely a ritualistic recitation of words, but a heartfelt conversation with our Heavenly Father. It's about opening our hearts and minds to Him, humbly acknowledging our dependence on Him, and earnestly seeking His wisdom and direction. Prayer should be a consistent practice, a daily dialogue that cultivates intimacy with God. It's in these moments of quiet reflection and open communication that we are most receptive to His voice.

Effective prayer involves more than simply listing our wants and needs. It requires listening—a willingness to hear God's response, which may not always come in the way we expect. Sometimes, His answer is a gentle nudge, a subtle prompting of the Spirit. Other times, it may be a clear and resounding "yes" or "no." Learning to discern His voice requires practice, patience, and a reliance on the His spirit. We must cultivate a quiet spirit, free from distractions, allowing ourselves to be truly present in the moment of prayer.

As we pray, seeking God's guidance, we must be mindful of our posture of heart. Humility is crucial. We should approach God with a spirit of openness and receptiveness, acknowledging our limitations and dependence on Him. Pride can blind us to His guidance, while humility opens our hearts to His wisdom and direction. We must be willing to surrender our own will to His, trusting that His plan for our lives is far greater than anything we could devise on our own.

Beyond prayer, diligent study of God's Word is essential for seeking His guidance. The Bible is not simply a historical document; it's a living and active source of truth, wisdom, and guidance. Through consistent Bible study, we become familiar with

God's character, His promises, and His principles. This knowledge equips us to discern His voice and understand His will for our lives.

Reading Scripture is just the beginning; the key is to meditate on what we read, allowing God's Word to penetrate our hearts and minds. We should ask ourselves how the passages we are reading apply to our lives, seeking to understand their practical implications. Journaling our thoughts and reflections can help to deepen our understanding and facilitate spiritual growth. Considering the historical context of the scriptures and understanding the original intent can enhance our comprehension and application of biblical principles. God's truth about us helps illuminate the truth and apply it meaningfully to our personal circumstances.

Beyond personal Bible study, engaging in group Bible studies can offer valuable insights and perspectives. Discussing scriptures with other believers, sharing different interpretations, and engaging in collaborative reflection can broaden our understanding and provide valuable support. The fellowship of believers is crucial, providing accountability and encouragement in our journey of faith. It's within a supportive Christian community that we can learn to seek God's guidance collectively and to apply it practically to our daily lives.

Seeking wise counsel is another vital aspect of seeking God's guidance. This doesn't mean seeking advice from everyone we know; rather, it's about seeking counsel from mature, godly individuals who can offer guidance rooted in biblical principles. These could be pastors, mentors, or trusted friends who are further along in their faith journey. They can provide an objective perspective, offer encouragement, and hold us accountable in our pursuit of God's will. Choosing our advisors wisely is crucial; we should seek counsel from individuals known for their wisdom, integrity, and spiritual discernment.

It's important to discern between seeking advice and seeking validation. Seeking validation often stems from insecurity and a desire for external approval. Seeking advice, however, is a humble request for guidance and wisdom. We must approach our advisors with a teachable spirit, open to feedback and willing to learn from their experience. We should seek those who will challenge us to grow spiritually and who will speak truth in love. Listening to and receiving constructive criticism is pivotal for growth and spiritual maturity. However, we must still filter all advice through the lens of scripture, ensuring it aligns with God's Word and our own conscience.

Sometimes, God's guidance comes through unexpected circumstances or difficult situations. These trials can be refining fires, shaping us into the individuals He desires us to be. While we may not always understand His reasons, we can trust that He is working all things together for good for those who love Him (Romans 8:28). Through these challenging experiences, we may discover hidden strengths, develop greater resilience, and gain a deeper understanding of God's character and His love for us.

Developing spiritual disciplines is integral to cultivating a heart sensitive to God's guidance. Fasting, for example, can create spiritual space and enhance our sensitivity to God. Quiet time, dedicated to prayer and meditation, fosters an intimacy with God that enables us to hear His voice more clearly. Regular attendance at church services provides opportunities for fellowship, worship, and receiving instruction from God's Word. These disciplines are not merely religious rituals; they are spiritual practices that strengthen our relationship with God and enhance our ability to receive His guidance.

Remember, seeking God's guidance is not a one-time event; it's a lifelong pursuit. It's a journey of faith that involves continuous learning, growth, and dependence on God. There will be times of clarity and times of uncertainty, moments of profound insight and periods of questioning. The key is to persevere, trusting in God's faithfulness and His unwavering love. As we actively seek His guidance, He will equip us with the wisdom, strength, and direction we need to fulfill His purpose for our lives. The journey may be challenging, but the reward is a life lived in His perfect will, filled with purpose, meaning, and joy.

God's plan for our lives is not a rigid formula, but a dynamic and evolving process. His guidance is often revealed incrementally, step by step, as we walk in obedience to His commands. He doesn't necessarily reveal the entire blueprint of our lives at once, but rather guides us along the path, revealing His will for us as we journey. This trust in His timing and His process is crucial. We must learn to discern His gentle nudges and to recognize His voice amidst the noise of life.

In closing, remember that seeking God's guidance is an act of faith, a constant surrender to His will. It involves a willingness to listen, to learn, and to obey. It is a journey of humility, recognizing our limitations and dependence on God. It requires patience, understanding that God's timing is not always our timing. And finally, it necessitates perseverance, knowing that the reward of a life lived in God's purpose far outweighs any challenges we may encounter along the way. Embrace this journey, trust in His guidance, and allow Him to lead you to the life He has designed for you.

Living Your Purpose

Having explored the methods of discerning God's purpose, the crucial next step is to actively live it out. This isn't merely a passive acceptance of a divine blueprint; it's a dynamic engagement, a daily commitment to aligning your actions with the will of God. This requires faith, courage, and a willingness to step outside your comfort zone, trusting that God will provide the necessary strength and guidance along the way. Remember, discovering your purpose is only half the battle; living it out is where the true transformation takes place.

The first step in living out your purpose is to identify your spiritual gifts and talents. These are not merely skills or abilities; they are gifts bestowed upon you by the Holy Ghost, uniquely designed to equip you for service within the body of Christ. Take time for introspection, reflecting on your natural inclinations, the things that excite and energize you, and the areas where you feel a sense of calling. Pray for clarity, asking God to reveal the specific talents He has placed within you. Seek feedback from trusted friends, mentors, or pastors; they may have observed abilities in you that you haven't fully recognized. Remember the parable of the talents (Matthew 25:14-30); God entrusts us with gifts, expecting us to utilize them for His glory.

Once you've identified your spiritual gifts, the next step is to discover how to apply them in service to others. This might involve volunteering at a local church or charity, using your skills to mentor others, or sharing your faith through evangelism. The possibilities are limitless, reflecting the diversity of God's gifts and the vast needs within the world. Don't be afraid to step outside your comfort zone; God often calls us to places and tasks that stretch us beyond our perceived limitations. Embrace these challenges as opportunities for growth and spiritual development. Through serving others, you not only fulfill God's purpose for your life but also experience the immense joy and fulfillment that comes from making a positive impact.

Consider your unique personality and circumstances. God's purpose is not a one-size-fits-all approach. He has intricately designed each individual, creating unique gifts and talents suited to their personality and life context. What works for one person may not work for another. Embrace your individuality, recognizing that your unique contribution is essential to the grand tapestry of God's work. Your passions, strengths, and experiences should be integrated into how you live out your purpose. Don't try to force yourself into a mold that doesn't fit; instead, allow God to guide you into the roles and responsibilities that align with your unique gifts and circumstances.

Living out God's purpose often involves overcoming obstacles and facing challenges. This journey is rarely smooth; it's filled with ups and downs, moments of clarity and periods of doubt. However, remember that these challenges are not roadblocks but opportunities for growth. They test your faith, refine your character, and deepen your reliance on God. During challenging times, remember to lean on God's promises, seeking His strength and guidance through prayer and meditation on Scripture. Surround yourself with a supportive community of faith, drawing strength and encouragement from fellow believers. Remember that God never abandons His children; He walks with us through every trial, providing the support and grace we need to overcome any obstacle.

Trust in God's timing; He knows the perfect moment for everything. Don't get discouraged if your journey doesn't unfold as you anticipated. God's plan unfolds in His own time, according to His perfect will. It's important to trust in His timing and process, even when things seem slow or uncertain. Focus on faithfulness rather than success; when you are faithful in the small things, God will entrust you with greater responsibilities. Be patient, allowing God to orchestrate the circumstances of your life, guiding you step-by-step towards the fulfillment of His purpose.

Be prepared for adjustments along the way. God's guidance is not a static roadmap; it's a dynamic process, often requiring adjustments and recalibrations. As you progress, you may discover new aspects of your purpose, leading to changes in your direction or approach. Remain open to God's leading, being willing to adapt and adjust your plans as necessary. Flexibility and adaptability are key to navigating the twists and turns of this journey. Be willing to embrace new opportunities, even if they seem unexpected or challenging. Remember that God often works through unexpected circumstances to shape us and refine us for His purpose.

Cultivate perseverance; fulfilling God's purpose requires ongoing commitment. It's not a sprint but a marathon, requiring dedication, patience, and a steadfast heart. There will be times of discouragement and doubt, moments when you question your abilities and your calling. However, it's during these times that perseverance is most crucial. Draw strength from your faith, remembering God's promises and His unwavering love for you. Surround yourself with a community of faith that will encourage and support you along the way. Never give up on your journey; the rewards of fulfilling God's purpose far outweigh any challenges you may encounter.

One of the most vital aspects of living out your purpose is to focus on your impact on others. God's purpose is rarely about personal achievement; it's about serving others and making a positive impact on the world. Therefore, constantly evaluate your actions and their effect on those around you. Are you using your gifts and talents to build others up, to offer encouragement, and to make a difference in their lives? Do your actions reflect the love and compassion of Christ? This focus on others will keep you grounded and will help to ensure that your life reflects God's purpose.

Remember the importance of accountability. Share your journey with trusted friends, family, or mentors. Having individuals to hold you accountable will help to keep you focused and on track. They can provide support, guidance, and encouragement when you face challenges. This accountability can also prevent you from straying from God's purpose or from being sidetracked by worldly distractions. Choose your accountability partners wisely; select individuals who are committed to your spiritual growth and who will offer constructive feedback and support.

Finally, celebrate your victories along the way. Recognize and appreciate the progress you've made, the obstacles you've overcome, and the positive impact you've had on others. Acknowledge God's hand in your journey, giving Him the glory for every accomplishment. Celebrating your victories will help to boost your morale and encourage you to continue pressing forward. Remember that fulfilling God's purpose is a journey, not a destination; there will always be more to accomplish, more people to serve, and more opportunities to make a difference. Embrace each step of the journey, trusting in God's guidance and celebrating His blessings along the way. Living out God's purpose is a life-long journey, one that will continuously unfold as you remain faithful and obedient to His calling. It's a path of growth, service, and transformation, filled with challenges and rewards, all leading to a life of purpose, meaning, and joy.

Chapter 6

Moving Forward with Hope and Confidence

Embracing the freedom found in Christ means shedding the old, wounded self and stepping into a new identity defined by His grace and love. This isn't a simple switch; it's a transformative process that requires conscious effort, consistent prayer, and a deep reliance on God. This new identity isn't about pretending everything is perfect; it's about acknowledging past hurts while simultaneously embracing the healing power of God's forgiveness and grace. It's about acknowledging your past without letting it define your future.

The journey to reclaiming your identity begins with recognizing the lies that toxic relationships have whispered into your heart. These lies often center on your self-worth, your capabilities, and your value in God's eyes. You may have internalized messages that you are unworthy, unlovable, or incapable of building healthy relationships. These are not truths; they are distortions created by the toxic dynamics you've experienced.

Scripture provides a powerful antidote to these lies. Remember the words of Psalm 139:14: "I praise you because I am fearfully and wonderfully made; your works are wonderful, I know that full well." This verse reminds us that we are uniquely created by God, each with inherent worth and dignity. We are not mistakes; we are masterpieces crafted by a loving Creator. This understanding forms the foundation for building a new identity rooted in God's unconditional love.

Take time to actively challenge these negative self-perceptions. Write down the lies you've believed about yourself and then counter them with truths from Scripture. For example, if you believe you're unlovable, counter that with verses like 1 John 4:16: "And so we know and rely on the love God has for us. God is love. Whoever lives in love lives in God, and God in them." If you believe you're incapable of healthy relationships, remember that God desires to guide you towards healthy, fulfilling connections based on His principles.

Forgiveness plays a crucial role in this process. Forgiving those who have hurt you is not about condoning their actions; it's about releasing the bitterness and resentment that bind you to the past. Holding onto anger and unforgiveness keeps you chained to the toxicity you're trying to escape. It prevents you from experiencing the freedom and healing that God offers. Forgiveness is a gift you give yourself, allowing you to break free from the cycle of pain and move forward with hope. Remember, forgiveness is a process, not a single event. It requires consistent effort and a willingness to surrender your pain to God.

As you begin to forgive, you'll find yourself becoming more compassionate not only towards others, but also towards yourself. Self-compassion is vital in this journey of healing. Treat yourself with the same kindness and understanding you would offer a close friend facing similar struggles. Recognize that you've been through trauma and that it's okay to grieve, to feel pain, and to allow yourself time to heal.

One powerful tool in embracing your new identity is through positive affirmations. Repeatedly declaring truths about yourself based on God's Word can reprogram your subconscious mind and replace the negative self-talk with positive, life-giving messages. Start each day with affirmations like, "I am loved by God," "I am worthy of His love," "I am capable of building healthy relationships," and "I am strong and resilient." Speak these affirmations out loud, believing them in your heart.

Spiritual disciplines like prayer, meditation, and Bible study are essential in strengthening your new identity in Christ. Through prayer, you connect with God, allowing Him to fill you with His love, peace, and strength. Meditation on Scripture helps you internalize God's truth, shaping your thoughts and actions. Bible study equips you with the knowledge and wisdom you need to navigate life's challenges and to build a life founded on God's principles.

Surrounding yourself with a supportive community of faith is crucial. Connect with a church where you feel loved, accepted, and encouraged. Build relationships with people who understand what you're going through and who can offer support and accountability. Sharing your story with trusted friends can be incredibly liberating, helping you to process your emotions and to gain a new perspective. These connections provide a safe space for you to be vulnerable and to receive the love and encouragement you need.

Remember that building a new identity is an ongoing process. There will be setbacks along the way, moments when you doubt yourself and your progress. These moments are opportunities to lean on God's grace and to reaffirm your identity in Him. Don't be discouraged by these setbacks; celebrate your successes, no matter how small, and acknowledge God's hand in your healing journey.

Your identity in Christ is not based on your performance or your perfection; it's grounded in His unconditional love and grace.

Consider journaling as a way to document your progress and to process your emotions. Writing down your thoughts and feelings can be therapeutic, providing an outlet for your pain and allowing you to reflect on your growth. Review your journal entries periodically to track your progress and to remind yourself of how far you've come.

Engaging in activities that bring you joy and that nourish your soul is essential. This could involve spending time in nature, listening to uplifting music, reading inspiring books, or pursuing creative hobbies. These activities help you to reconnect with yourself and to rediscover the passions and interests that make you unique.

Living in Resilience

As you move forward, remember that your journey is not a race. Be patient and compassionate with yourself, recognizing that healing takes time. Embrace each step of the process, trusting in God's timing and His perfect plan for your life. Your new identity in Christ is not a destination but a continuous journey of growth, transformation, and deepening your relationship with God. Allow Him to mold you, shape you, and reveal the beautiful person He has created you to be.

Ultimately, embracing your new identity in Christ empowers you to build healthy relationships, to set boundaries, and to live a life of purpose and joy. It's a life characterized by freedom, peace, and a deep sense of self-worth rooted in God's unwavering love. It's a life where the pain of the past no longer defines you, but instead serves as a testament to God's remarkable power to heal and restore. Remember that you are not alone on this journey; God is with you every step of the way, guiding you, strengthening you, and leading you into a future filled with hope and promise. Trust in His plan, embrace His grace, and allow your new identity in Christ to flourish. This transformation is a gift from God, one that unlocks unimaginable potential and joy. Embrace it fully and watch as your life is transformed by the power of His love.

Cultivating resilience isn't about avoiding hardship; it's about facing it with unwavering faith and a spirit empowered by God's grace. The storms of life are inevitable, but our response to them shapes our character and deepens our relationship with the Divine. Building resilience is a spiritual practice, a conscious choice to trust in God's unwavering love and provision even amidst turmoil. This involves nurturing your inner strength, developing coping mechanisms rooted in biblical principles, and embracing a perspective that sees challenges not as insurmountable obstacles but as opportunities for growth and spiritual refinement.

One foundational element of resilience is a steadfast faith in God's sovereignty. Recognizing that God is in control, even when things seem chaotic or unjust, provides a profound sense of peace and stability. This understanding doesn't negate the pain or difficulty of a situation; rather, it anchors us to a truth larger than our circumstances. The book of Romans powerfully expresses this truth: "For I am convinced that neither death nor life, neither angels nor demons, neither the present nor the future, nor any powers, neither height nor depth, nor anything else in all creation, will be able to separate us from the love of God that is in Christ Jesus our Lord" (Romans 8:38-39). This verse underscores the unshakeable nature of God's love, offering a wall of defense against fear and despair.

Prayer becomes an invaluable tool in cultivating resilience. It's not merely a passive act of asking God for help; it's an active engagement with Him, a deepening of our relationship in times of trial. Through prayer, we pour out our hearts, sharing our anxieties, fears, and pain. We seek His guidance, strength, and wisdom to navigate difficult situations. Furthermore, prayer allows us to surrender our burdens to God, releasing the weight of our anxieties and trusting in His ability to carry us through. Remember Jesus' words in Matthew 6:34: "Therefore do not worry about tomorrow, for tomorrow will worry about itself. Each day has enough trouble of its own." This passage emphasizes the importance of focusing on the present moment, trusting in God's provision for each day's challenges.

Scripture offers a wellspring of wisdom and strength for building resilience. Regular Bible study helps us to internalize God's truths, providing a framework for understanding life's complexities. The Psalms, in particular, offer a powerful reflection of human experience, acknowledging both suffering and praise. Reading and meditating on these passages reminds us that we are not alone in our struggles; others before us have faced similar trials and found solace in their faith. Moreover, the stories of biblical heroes, like Joseph, David, and Esther, demonstrate the power of resilience in the face of immense adversity. These accounts teach us that even in the darkest moments, God remains faithful and works all things for the good of those who love Him (Romans 8:28).

Developing healthy coping mechanisms is another crucial aspect of building resilience. This involves identifying and addressing unhealthy coping strategies, such as isolation, substance abuse, or self-harm, and replacing them with healthier alternatives. These healthier strategies might include engaging in regular exercise, nurturing healthy relationships, practicing mindfulness or meditation, or pursuing creative outlets. These activities help us to manage stress, regulate our emotions, and promote overall well-being. The importance of community cannot be overstated. Surrounding ourselves with supportive individuals who offer encouragement, accountability, and understanding is vital in navigating difficult times. This could involve connecting with a supportive church community, engaging in small groups or mentoring relationships, or simply seeking out trusted friends or family members.

Forgiveness, both of ourselves and others, plays a crucial role in building resilience. Holding onto resentment and bitterness only perpetuates the pain and hinders our ability to move forward. Forgiving those who have hurt us is not about condoning their actions; it's about releasing the emotional burden that prevents healing and growth. Similarly, forgiving ourselves for past mistakes or shortcomings is essential for breaking free from self-condemnation and embracing God's grace. This process of forgiveness requires time, patience, and a willingness to surrender our pain to God. It's a spiritual act, freeing us from the chains of the past and empowering us to embrace a brighter future.

Self-compassion is another vital element of resilience. Treating ourselves with the same kindness and understanding we would offer a friend in need is crucial for navigating difficult times. This means acknowledging our pain, validating our emotions, and accepting that it's okay to not be okay. It's about recognizing our limitations and acknowledging the impact of past trauma without allowing it to define our present or future. Self-compassion fosters a sense of self-worth and empowers us to face challenges with greater grace and strength.

Positive self-talk, rooted in God's truth, can significantly impact our resilience. Replacing negative thoughts and self-criticism with positive affirmations based on Scripture can reprogram our minds and promote a healthier self-image. This practice reinforces our identity in Christ, reminding us of our inherent worth and God's unconditional love. Daily affirmations, such as "I am loved by

God," "I am strong in His strength," or "I am capable of overcoming this challenge," can reinforce our belief in our resilience and God's power within us.

Being mindful of our thoughts and meditating on what is right can help us cultivate resilience. Proverbs 2:10-13 states, "Wisdom enters your heart, and knowledge is pleasant to your soul; discretion will preserve you; understanding will keep you, delivering you from the way of evil and from the man who speaks perverse things." It's essential to be aware of our thoughts and to understand what God says to us for our well-being. Philippians 4:8 provides guidance on how to achieve this: "Finally, brethren, whatsoever things are true, whatsoever things are honest, whatsoever things are just, whatsoever things are pure, whatsoever things are lovely, whatsoever things are of good report; if there be any virtue, and if there be any praise, think on these things." When we focus on these qualities, we build resilience against the enemy's plots to destroy us.

Ultimately, cultivating resilience is a journey of faith, growth, and transformation. It's about actively engaging in spiritual disciplines, developing healthy coping mechanisms, and nurturing a deep relationship with God. It requires embracing our vulnerabilities, acknowledging our struggles, and trusting in God's unwavering love and provision. The path may not always be easy, but the rewards of a life lived with resilience, grounded in faith, are immeasurable. By embracing these principles, we can navigate life's inevitable challenges with hope, confidence, and an unwavering trust in the power of God to work all things together for good. The journey is one of continuous growth, allowing us to become more Christ-like, compassionate, and resilient with each challenge we overcome. We find not only personal strength, but also a deeper understanding of God's grace and the transformative power of His love.

Healthy Boundaries is Key

Maintaining healthy boundaries isn't a one-time event; it's a lifelong commitment, a daily practice woven into the fabric of our lives. Just as we nurture our physical health through consistent exercise and diet, we must consistently nurture our emotional and spiritual well-being by upholding our boundaries. This requires ongoing vigilance, self-awareness, and a steadfast commitment to prioritizing our needs.

One of the most crucial aspects of long-term boundary maintenance is consistent self-care. This isn't about selfish indulgence; it's about recognizing that we cannot pour from an empty cup. If we are depleted emotionally, spiritually, or physically, our ability to set and maintain boundaries will inevitably weaken. Self-care, therefore, becomes a foundational pillar upon which our boundary system rests.

This self-care routine should be personalized and tailored to your individual needs. It might include regular exercise, mindful meditation, spending time in nature, engaging in hobbies that bring joy, or simply setting aside time for quiet reflection and prayer. The key is to identify activities that replenish your energy and restore your sense of self. Perhaps it involves joining a supportive book club, engaging in a craft you enjoy, or taking a relaxing bath. The specific activities are less important than the consistent commitment to prioritizing self-nurturing activities.

Importantly, self-care should also encompass setting healthy limits on your time and energy. Learning to say "no" to requests that drain your resources or compromise your well-being is essential. This doesn't mean being unkind or uncooperative; it's about recognizing your limitations and protecting your energy for those things that truly matter. Remember, saying "no" to one thing often opens up space to say "yes" to something more meaningful and aligned with your values.

Consistent communication is another vital component of maintaining healthy boundaries long-term. This means clearly and assertively communicating your needs, expectations, and limits to others. This may involve setting clear expectations in relationships, defining personal space, or establishing boundaries regarding work or social commitments. It's essential to be direct, honest, and respectful in your communication, while remaining firm in upholding your boundaries.

Avoid vague or passive-aggressive language. Instead, use "I" statements to express your needs and feelings without blaming or accusing others. For example, instead of saying "You always interrupt me," you might say, "I feel unheard when I'm interrupted. Could you please let me finish my thought before speaking?" This approach encourages understanding and collaboration, rather than defensiveness and conflict.

Remember that communication is a two-way street. It's not just about expressing your own needs; it's also about actively listening to and understanding the perspectives of others. However, this listening should not compromise your boundaries. If someone is consistently disregarding your boundaries, despite your clear communication, it may be necessary to re-evaluate the relationship or set even stronger limits.

Coping with boundary challenges is an inevitable part of maintaining healthy boundaries long-term. There will be times when others test your limits, misunderstand your needs, or intentionally disregard your boundaries. Having a plan in place for managing these challenges is crucial. This might involve having pre-determined responses ready for common boundary violations or identifying supportive individuals who can offer guidance and encouragement.

Prayer and meditation are powerful tools for navigating boundary challenges. When faced with a situation that threatens to compromise your boundaries, taking time to pray for guidance and strength can provide the clarity and resilience you need to respond effectively. Meditation can help calm your emotions and center you in the present moment, allowing you to respond thoughtfully rather than reactively.

Self-Reflection

Seeking guidance from a trusted mentor, counselor, or pastor can provide invaluable support and perspective. They can offer objective advice, help you process difficult emotions, and provide accountability as you navigate challenges. A support system provides a crucial safety net during these challenging times. They can offer encouragement, understanding, and practical strategies for managing difficult situations. Remember that seeking help is a sign of strength, not weakness.

Regular self-reflection is key to maintaining healthy boundaries over time. Periodically assess how your boundaries are working, identify areas where adjustments may be needed, and make necessary changes. This ongoing process of self-evaluation is essential for ensuring that your boundaries remain effective and supportive of your well-being. Ask yourself: Are my boundaries clear? Are they being respected? Am I communicating my needs effectively? Am I prioritizing my well-being?

Journaling can be a powerful tool for self-reflection. Regularly writing about your experiences, feelings, and observations can provide valuable insights into your boundary-setting practices. It allows you to track your progress, identify patterns, and make adjustments as needed. This creates a valuable record of your journey, allowing you to see the growth and progress you have made.

Learning to forgive both yourself and others is crucial for long-term boundary maintenance. It's easy to get discouraged when boundaries are challenged, or even to blame yourself for not setting them effectively initially. Forgiveness allows you to release resentment and move forward with renewed energy and determination. Remember God's unfailing forgiveness and extend that grace to yourself and others.

Forgiveness doesn't mean condoning harmful behavior; it means releasing the emotional burden you carry, allowing yourself to heal and move on. Forgiving those who have crossed your boundaries doesn't necessitate continuing the relationship in the same way. It allows you to find peace and move forward with your life, without being held captive by past hurts. It's crucial to remember that forgiveness is a process, not a destination, and that seeking help in the forgiveness process can be immensely beneficial.

Maintaining healthy boundaries is an ongoing process that requires consistent effort, self-awareness, and a commitment to prioritizing your well-being. By incorporating these strategies into your life, you can build resilience, protect your emotional health, and cultivate relationships that are both supportive and respectful. Remember, the journey toward healthy boundaries is a testament to your self-worth and a reflection of your commitment to honoring God's design for your life. The rewards—a life lived with greater peace, purpose, and confidence—are immeasurable. Embrace the journey, knowing that God's grace and strength will sustain you every step of the way. He will equip you with the tools and the strength to navigate any challenge you face. Your journey is a reflection of God's work in your life, and you are never alone in this process.

Building a strong support system is not a luxury; it's a necessity, particularly as you navigate the complexities of healing from toxic relationships and establishing healthy boundaries. The journey toward emotional and spiritual wholeness is rarely a solitary one. Scripture itself repeatedly emphasizes the importance of community, reminding us that we are not meant to walk alone. Proverbs 17:17 states, "A friend loves at all times, and a brother is born for adversity." This verse speaks volumes about the enduring power of supportive relationships, especially during times of trial and tribulation.

The foundation of a healthy support system rests upon the bedrock of faith. Surrounding yourself with individuals who share your beliefs and values can provide a unique level of understanding, encouragement, and accountability. This is not about finding people who perfectly mirror your life; rather, it's about finding those who offer genuine support, challenge you to grow, and hold you accountable to your commitment to healing.

One of the most significant components of a robust support system is a mentor. A mentor is someone who has walked a similar path, offering wisdom, guidance, and a listening ear. They are individuals who can provide perspective, offer insights gleaned from their own experiences, and help you avoid potential pitfalls. A mentor isn't necessarily someone older or more experienced in years; rather, it's someone who possesses a deeper understanding of spiritual principles and the challenges you face. Finding a mentor could involve seeking out a pastor, a trusted elder in your church, a spiritual advisor, or even a fellow believer who has successfully navigated similar circumstances. The key is to find someone whose life reflects the values and principles you admire.

The role of a mentor extends beyond simply offering advice. They are there to provide emotional support, a safe space to share your struggles, and celebrate your victories. They can help you to process difficult emotions, challenge negative thought patterns, and reaffirm your faith when doubt arises. Mentorship requires mutual respect, open communication, and a willingness to learn from each other.

Beyond a mentor, cultivating accountability partners is essential. These are individuals who will support you in your commitment to maintaining boundaries and pursuing emotional healing. Accountability partners are crucial for staying focused on your goals and providing consistent encouragement during challenging times. They offer a space for honest self-reflection, offering a different perspective on your challenges and progress. They provide a safe space where you can confess struggles, share victories, and receive much-needed support and encouragement.

This accountability isn't about judgment or criticism; it's about mutual support and encouragement. Find individuals who will celebrate your successes and offer gentle guidance during setbacks. They should be people who genuinely care about your well-being and are willing to invest their time and energy in your healing journey. Choosing accountability partners requires discernment, selecting people who will offer honest feedback without being judgmental. Their role is to encourage, challenge, and support your growth, not to condemn or criticize.

Joining a supportive spiritual community is another vital step in building a strong support system. This could be your local church, a small group study, or a faith-based support group specifically designed for individuals recovering from toxic relationships. The shared faith and understanding within such communities can provide a sense of belonging, acceptance, and encouragement that is invaluable during the healing process. These communities offer opportunities for fellowship, prayer, and shared experiences, fostering a sense of community and mutual support. You will find people who understand your struggle, offering empathy and shared experiences. Such environments can be powerfully therapeutic.

Within these communities, you can participate in activities that nurture your spiritual well-being, such as prayer meetings, Bible studies, and service projects. These activities not only strengthen your faith but also provide opportunities to connect with others on a deeper level, creating a network of support and understanding. Participation in these activities often leads to the formation of close, meaningful relationships built upon shared faith and mutual respect.

It's important to remember that building a support system is an ongoing process. It requires intentionality, effort, and a willingness to be vulnerable and open. Don't hesitate to reach out to others, share your experiences, and seek the help you need. Remember that God has placed people in your life for a purpose, and part of that purpose may be to provide the support and encouragement you need to heal and thrive.

Cultivating a strong support system also involves discerning who you surround yourself with. Just as it's important to build relationships with positive influences, it's equally essential to identify and limit contact with those who might hinder your progress. This might involve setting boundaries with individuals who consistently drain your energy or reinforce negative thought patterns. This isn't about cutting people out of your life; rather, it's about protecting your emotional and spiritual well-being by creating distance from those who may not be supportive of your healing journey. This may involve limiting contact, or in more severe cases, completely severing the relationship.

Prayer and meditation are invaluable tools in building and nurturing your support system. Through prayer, you can seek God's guidance in identifying individuals who can provide genuine support and protection. You can also pray for wisdom and discernment in choosing your mentors and accountability partners. Meditation can help you cultivate inner peace and resilience, enabling you to approach relationships with greater clarity and emotional stability.

Remember, your support system shouldn't be static; it should evolve as you grow and change. As your healing journey progresses, your needs may shift, requiring you to adjust your support system accordingly. This might involve adding new relationships, strengthening existing ones, or letting go of those that no longer serve you. This process is dynamic, a reflection of your growth and evolving needs.

Building a strong support system is a testament to your commitment to your healing and your growth. It demonstrates a recognition of your need for community and a willingness to accept help. It's a sign of strength, not weakness. By actively seeking and nurturing supportive relationships, you are investing in your future, creating a foundation upon which you can build a life of hope, confidence, and lasting peace. God has not called us to walk this journey alone; He has provided a community of believers to support us, lift us, and guide us on the path to wholeness. Embrace this community, and allow it to strengthen and enrich your life. Remember that God's love and grace are always present, sustaining you through every step of your journey. This is a journey of faith, resilience, and profound transformation. Lean into the support around you, and experience the transformative power of God's grace working through your life and the lives of those who support you. Your journey is not a solitary one; it's a shared journey of faith and hope. Embrace it fully.

Having established the crucial role of a supportive community in your healing journey, we now turn our attention to the ultimate goal: living a life of purpose and joy, a life deeply rooted in your relationship with God. This is not merely the absence of toxicity; it's the active pursuit of a life brimming with meaning, fulfillment, and the unwavering peace that only God can provide. The challenges you've overcome, the boundaries you've established, and the support system you've cultivated are all stepping stones on this path towards a life defined by God's purpose and overflowing with His joy.

Purpose Filled Life

The Bible consistently emphasizes the importance of knowing and fulfilling God's purpose for your life. Jeremiah 29:11 reminds us, "For I know the plans I have for you," declares the Lord, "plans to prosper you and not to harm you, plans to give you hope and a future." This powerful verse isn't a passive promise; it's an invitation to actively seek and discover the unique path God has laid out for you. This involves prayerful reflection, seeking guidance from scripture, and listening to the gentle promptings of God's words that you have planted within your heart.

Discovering your purpose isn't necessarily a sudden epiphany; it's often a gradual process of discernment and growth. It involves identifying your talents, passions, and gifts and aligning them with God's overarching plan. Consider the various areas of your life: your professional pursuits, your relationships, your spiritual practices, and your service to others. Where do you feel a deep sense of calling, a compelling urge to contribute your unique abilities to the world? These are potential indicators of God's purpose for your life.

This process requires a willingness to be vulnerable and open to God's guidance. It means being willing to step outside of your comfort zone, to embrace new challenges and opportunities, and to trust that God will equip you with everything you need to succeed. It involves asking yourself tough questions: What are my deepest desires? What are my strengths and weaknesses? How can I use my gifts to serve others and bring glory to God?

A crucial aspect of living a purposeful life is cultivating gratitude. Focusing on the blessings in your life, both big and small, shifts your perspective from lack to abundance. It fosters a heart of thankfulness, allowing you to appreciate the journey, even amidst challenges. Expressing gratitude through prayer, journaling, or simply verbalizing your appreciation to God and others reinforces the positive aspects of your life, building resilience and fostering contentment. Cultivating a grateful heart is an act of spiritual discipline that strengthens your connection with God and enhances your overall well-being.

Alongside purpose, joy is an essential element of a life pleasing to God. This isn't a fleeting emotion; it's a deep-seated peace and contentment that stems from a right relationship with God. It's the joy that surpasses understanding, the joy that endures even in the midst of trials and tribulations. Galatians 5:22-23 describes the fruit of the Spirit, including "joy" amongst love, peace, patience, kindness, goodness, faithfulness, gentleness, and self-control. This passage illustrates that joy is not merely a feeling; it's a characteristic of a life lived in accordance with God's will.

The pursuit of joy often involves intentional choices: prioritizing meaningful relationships, engaging in activities that bring you fulfillment, and making time for rest and rejuvenation. It's about actively nurturing your spiritual, emotional, and physical well-being, creating a balanced life that honors God and reflects your commitment to a healthy lifestyle. This might involve setting aside dedicated time for prayer, meditation, or Bible study, engaging in activities you find enjoyable, and ensuring you prioritize adequate sleep, healthy eating, and regular exercise.

Remember the importance of forgiveness, both of yourself and others. Holding onto resentment and bitterness only hinders your ability to experience true joy. Forgiveness isn't condoning harmful behavior; it's releasing the burden of anger and bitterness that weighs heavily on your heart and spirit. It allows you to move forward, free from the shackles of the past, and embrace the healing power of God's grace. This act of releasing hurt and anger is vital to the journey towards emotional wholeness.

Forgiveness extends to yourself as well. You may carry self-blame and regret from past experiences. God's grace extends fully to you, encompassing forgiveness and healing. Acknowledge your mistakes, learn from them, and extend compassion to yourself, as you would to another experiencing similar struggles. Release the self-criticism and embrace God's unconditional love.

Building healthy relationships is also integral to experiencing true joy. Now that you've established healthy boundaries and cultivated a strong support system, focus on nurturing those relationships that enrich your life. Choose to surround yourself with people who uplift and encourage you, who share your values, and who support your growth in Christ. This includes maintaining open communication, actively listening to others, and offering support and understanding in return.

Remember, building relationships takes time and effort. It requires a willingness to be vulnerable, to share your thoughts and feelings honestly, and to forgive when necessary. It means being intentional in your interactions, seeking opportunities to connect with others, and nurturing the bonds you cherish. Prioritizing healthy relationships is a testament to your commitment to building a life rich in love and belonging.

Finally, living a life of purpose and joy is not a destination; it's a journey. There will be challenges and setbacks along the way, but with God's guidance and support, you can navigate them with hope and confidence. Remember the lessons you've learned, the strength you've gained, and the support system you've cultivated. These are invaluable resources as you continue to grow and evolve in your faith.

Your journey of healing and transformation isn't over; it's a continuous process of learning, growth, and deepening your relationship with God. Embrace the challenges that lie ahead, knowing that God is with you every step of the way. Continue to seek His guidance, cultivate gratitude, prioritize your well-being, and nurture your relationships. As you do, you will discover the profound joy and fulfillment that come from living a life aligned with God's purpose.

To further support your continued growth, I encourage you to explore the following resources: If you know someone who needs immediate help, please call the National Hotline at 800-799-7233 or text "BEGIN" to 88788. You can also visit their website at thehotline.org. If you are interested in growing in Christ, visit me on YouTube by searching www.youtube.com/@karengaines272. You can also email me at karenplessgaines@outlook.com. Please include the title of this book in the subject line. I want to encourage you to read your Bible. If you don't have one and need assistance obtaining one, please email me at the address above and write "Need Bible" in the subject line. I would love to hear your story, so feel free to reach out anytime for guidance, prayer, or friendship.

Remember, God's love for you is unconditional, and He has a wonderful plan for your life. Trust in His promises and embrace the journey with hope, confidence, and unwavering faith. Your future is bright, filled with purpose, joy, and the abundant blessings of a life in Christ. The journey may have been difficult, but the destination—a life overflowing with God's love—is well worth the effort.

I sincerely hope that these pages have equipped you with the understanding needed to embrace and build upon God's words, enabling you to embark on a journey of healing from within. Be intentional about the company you keep—take a moment to assess those around you. Establish boundaries that ensure you are treated with respect, and don't hesitate to distance yourself from anyone who doesn't uplift you. Remember, God designed you for greatness! Allow His words to surround you and inspire you to awaken the Woman of Valor that resides within. Your journey to transformation starts now.

Chapter 7

Real Life Stories

The stories you are about to read come from courageous women who have defied the odds and escaped the suffocating grip of toxic relationships. While not every story has a happy ending, mine came dangerously close to tragedy.

After enduring six years of relentless abuse, my turning point arrived one fateful night when he pointed a gun at my head and pulled the trigger—it misfired. In that moment, I realized that God had spared my life.

I may not fully understand why others haven't experienced the same fortune, but I want you to know this: I am here for you every step of the way. My journey is not merely a story; it's a powerful testament to hope and resilience for anyone seeking a way out. Remember, you are not alone in this struggle. Together, we can find a path forward.

Now let me introduce you to Marta, Emma, and Sophie…

Marta

Marta sat on the edge of her bed, the faint light of dawn filtering through the curtains, casting soft shadows around her dimly lit room. She felt a familiar pang in her chest, a blend of anxiety and longing that had become her morning ritual for as long as she could remember. Across the room, her phone buzzed, a reminder of the world waiting for her beyond the walls of her isolation. But she hesitated, knowing whose message would appear.

Where are you?" Paul had texted, the words dripping with an urgency that always pulled at her heart. It wasn't just the anxiety of his tone; it was the weight of the lies that had woven themselves into the very fabric of their lives. And Marta believed them.

For four years, she had been romanticizing the beginning of their relationship. He had been passionate, caring, the kind of man who seemed to know her every thought. But as time passed, his gentle touch morphed into controlling gripped hands, and the sweet whispers turned into harsh criticisms that echoed in her mind long after he had spoken them. The "I love yous" became conditional, warped by the shadows of jealousy and anger that crept in uninvited.

Marta had spent countless nights convincing herself that things would change. "He's under stress," she'd tell her friends when they expressed concern. "He loves me; he just gets angry sometimes." The lies stacked upon one another, forming a wall so high that she couldn't see the sky. The truth of his manipulation—the choices he stripped away from her—became buried beneath layers of justifications.

It didn't take long for friends to fade away, one by one. They didn't understand her loyalty, her commitment to a love that felt more like a leash. Each time she turned to them, trying to share her pain, they offered concerned looks and gentle suggestions to leave. But Marta felt a sense of duty, a responsibility for the man she had committed to—after all, he said he would change, that things would get better.

But today felt different. The lies were beginning to unravel, as though a thin thread had snapped, exposing the gaping wounds they had concealed. She thought of her sister, Elena, who had reached out repeatedly, begging her to see the truth. "Marta, you deserve better. You're not happy," she had pleaded during their last call.

Elena's words replayed in her mind, louder now than the whispers of doubt Paul had instilled in her. The thought of escaping twisted inside her, a paradox of fear and relief. What if she left? Would she really find the strength to sever the ties that had become so entangled in her heart?

Marta glanced at her phone again; this time, fear gripped her. She imagined Paul's face twisted in anger, the ways he could threaten her and shame her for even contemplating leaving. "You'll ruin everything," he would say. "What about your family? They won't understand." Each thought felt like a dagger, carefully aimed to pierce her resolve.

But as she sat there, she remembered the weight of silence in her home, the nights filled with arguments that felt like suffocation. She thought of her sister, the comfort of her genuine concern, and the way Elena had always believed in her ability to find happiness. The thought spread warmth through her body.

Taking a deep breath, Marta reached for her phone. She hesitated, then began to type:

"Paul, I need to talk. Things can't continue like this. I'm unhappy."

As she hit send, she felt a rush of fear followed by an exhilarating sense of clarity. In that moment, she realized that the lies he had woven around her were not truths but traps. No longer would she allow herself to be defined by another's anger, nor would she let fear dictate her choices.

She needed to fight. Not just for herself but for the life that waited for her beyond this toxicity. She could hear her sister's voice now, clear and hopeful, and with it came the realization that the only things she had to lose were the chains that had bound her for so long.

With a renewed sense of purpose, Marta allowed the sunlight to wash over her, illuminating the path ahead. The road would be difficult, but for the first time in years, she believed in her own strength—strength enough to face the truth and to finally embrace the freedom she longed for.

Marta sat on the edge of her bed, clutching her phone tightly in her palm. The silence of the room felt deafening, punctuated only by the distant sounds of traffic outside her window. Her heart raced as she replayed the conversation in her mind, each word echoing sharply, reminding her of the bitterness that had seeped into their relationship.

When her phone rang almost immediately after she sent the text, a sense of dread washed over her. She hesitated, her finger hovering over the screen. Finally, she braced herself, pushed the button, and forced a smile into her voice, "That is the quickest you have ever responded to my messages."

Paul's voice dripped with sarcasm. "You said you need to talk, so talk."

His tone stung. Despite their history, she hadn't expected the anger to be so palpable through the line. "And why are you not happy? All you do is sit home all day doing whatever it is that you do."

Marta felt a lump form in her throat. She couldn't speak. The words were jumbled in her mind, tangled like the cords of her forgotten charger. She knew talking over the phone was safer than encountering Paul in person; the last time they were face-to-face, his hands had been unforgiving. She remembered the bruise he left on her arm, the way he had shouted, each word a bullet aimed at her heart. It was easier to hide behind the screen, but it didn't mean it was painless.

"Well?" he pressed again, impatience lacing his voice.

Taking a deep breath, she finally managed to say, "I'm going to stay with my sister for a while. I think I—we could use the break."

"What do you need a break from?" His voice was dangerously low now, the words unraveling like a threat. "You better be home when I get there—do you hear me?"

Her resolve cracked beneath the weight of his demand. A tear slipped down her cheek, and she brushed it away hastily with the back of her hand. "Yes, I hear you," she whispered, feeling small and insignificant, as if his anger could erase her very existence.

And just like that, he ended the call, leaving her in the uncomfortable silence that followed. What should she do? The question hung in the air, twisting her stomach in knots. Staying would mean grappling with his rage, enduring the walls closing in around her. But leaving — would that awaken the beast within him? Would fleeing ignite his fury in ways she couldn't predict?

Marta quietly set her phone down, her reflection catching her eye in the dresser mirror. What she saw was a shadow of the vibrant person she used to be. Her eyes were haunted, fatigue etched into her features. She thought of her sister, of the laughter they once shared, of the safety and warmth that now seemed like a distant memory.

With a firm grip on her decision, Marta began to pack a small overnight bag. A few changes of clothes, her favorite book, and a photograph of the two of them on a beach, carefree and blissful. As she zipped it shut, she felt a flicker of hope spark within her.

Once her bag was ready, she glanced around the room, taking in the remnants of her life with Paul — the framed photos, the gifts he had given her, the memories that were now tainted. It was time to reclaim her space, to carve out a new existence, even if it was filled with uncertainty.

Taking a deep breath, Marta quietly slipped out of the house, the door creaking only slightly as she shut it behind her. She drove toward her sister's home, each mile feeling like she was shedding the weight of fear. Adrenaline coursed through her veins, battling the remnants of doubt that clung to her. As she pulled into her sister's driveway, the warmth of familiarity enveloped her. She got out, clutching her bag tightly and walking toward the front door. Before she knocked, she felt a moment of clarity wash over her.

"I deserve better," she whispered to herself, knowing that this journey was about more than just a physical location. It was about breaking free, about taking the first steps toward a life unfettered by fear.

When her sister opened the door, the worry on her face turned to relief, and Marta stepped inside, leaving the past behind.

For the first time in a long while, she felt a spark of freedom. The road ahead was unwritten, but it was hers to explore.

Emma

Emma had always been the type of person who saw the silver lining in every cloud. Her bright smile and optimistic outlook on life had drawn people to her, but she didn't always see the darkness lurking in her own relationships. When she met Ryan, his charismatic personality and seemingly perfect facade enveloped her like a warm blanket. At first, he made her feel like the only person in the world, showering her with compliments and affection. But as their relationship deepened, the edges began to fray.

It started as small lies—harmless, she thought. "You're the only one I've ever loved," he would say, a statement that felt like the ultimate validation. Emma didn't realize it then, but that lie would stretch into a web of deceit that would ensnare her.

At first, the little warnings were easy to brush off. When Ryan made sarcastic comments about her friends or belittled her desire to pursue art, she convinced herself that he only wanted what was best for her. "He just wants me to succeed," she would tell herself, each time ignoring the unsettling feeling that nestled in her gut. But over time, these comments grew sharper, cutting deeper into her self-esteem until she felt like she was walking on eggshells.

The turning point came one stormy night when Emma returned home to find Ryan in a fit of rage. She had gone out with friends, a rare occurrence he had reluctantly agreed to; his grip on her social life had slowly tightened, but she felt safe, believing she could have a little freedom. Yet, when she opened the door, the atmosphere was charged with resentment.

"Do you think they care about you?" he growled, his voice thick with anger. "They're just using you for their own benefit. You're better off with me." As she stood frozen, the lies folded around her like a noose—the truth that she had lost herself in trying to please him. She had been made to feel unworthy of love outside his possessive grasp.

In the weeks that followed, Emma felt as if she were caught in a relentless storm, swept away by guilt and manipulation. Every time she mustered the courage to assert her independence, Ryan was there to reel her back in. They would sit on the worn couch in their small, cluttered apartment, the air thick with tension. "I only want what's best for you," he would insist, his voice a mix of sweetness and a dangerous edge. "You know I love you, right?"

His words, once comforting, began to weigh on her like an anchor. Every promise he made seemed to wrap around her heart like a noose. The fear that tangled in her thoughts grew insidious—was he really right about her friends? She remembered the way he twisted every story about them, painting them as opportunistic and untrustworthy. "They don't care about you, Emma," he would say, his eyes intense and searching. "They're just using you."

With each twisted truth, Emma felt her world contract, isolating her in a bubble of doubt. Time slipped through her fingers as sleepless nights turned into long days. She lay in bed, staring at the ceiling, her mind replaying moments of laughter that had filled her life before Ryan's influence loomed dark. Each fond memory crumbled under the weight of despair—a heavy reminder of how different things had been.

The lies which once felt like threads of connection now twisted and knotted deep within her, pressing against her chest until it was hard to breathe. Emma realized she could no longer distinguish love from control; they had become hopelessly intertwined in a volatile dance. The passion that had once ignited her spirit now brushed against her like fire, burning where it should have warmed.

Though she often felt like a prisoner in a gilded cage built by her own heart, sparks of rebellion flickered within her. It was during one of those suffocating nights that Emma resolved to confront Ryan. She couldn't keep living in fear, held captive by his twisted logic. As the sun dipped below the horizon, she steeled herself, hoping that this time would be different.

"Ryan," she began, her voice barely above a whisper, trembling as she collected her thoughts. "I need to talk about what's been happening between us."

He stiffened, the warmth fading from his expression as he leaned forward, eyes narrowing. "What do you mean, 'what's been happening'? You're just feeling confused, Emma. I'm only trying to protect you."

"No!" she interjected, surprising herself with the forcefulness in her voice. "I'm tired of feeling guilty for wanting my own space, my own friends. I need support, not control. This isn't love; it feels more like a prison."

For a moment, silence reigned in the room. Ryan's face was a mix of disbelief and wounded pride. "You think I'm trying to control you?" he asked, voice trembling. It was a dangerous question laced with accusation.

"Yes," she replied, heart racing. "You use your love as a weapon, and I can't keep living like this."

As she spoke, something within her shifted. It was as if the chains binding her spirit began to crack. She felt a surge of clarity wash over her, illuminating the shadows of doubt lingering in her mind. Maybe her friends did care. Maybe she didn't have to live in

Ryan's world of twisted truths. Seeing the anger flare up in his eyes, fear crept back into her heart. Yet within the fear was a burgeoning courage. Emma took a deep breath, grounding herself in the truth she had almost forgotten. "I'm leaving, Ryan."

In that moment, everything changed. The cage that had felt insurmountable suddenly seemed smaller, the bars weaker. With one courageous step toward her independence, Emma felt the first stirrings of hope within her again. It wouldn't be easy, but she was ready to fight for her freedom, for the laughter that once filled her life, and for a love that didn't come with chains. She would no longer be a prisoner in her own heart.

SOPHIE

Sophie had always been the light in every room she entered. Her laughter was infectious, a melody woven into the fabric of her friendships. But beneath her vibrant exterior lay a tumultuous world, one that the shadows of a toxic relationship had steadily eroded. It began harmlessly enough with Liam, whose charm and confidence swept her off her feet. At first, he worshiped her, and those early moments felt like a fairy tale. Yet, as time passed, the fabric of their love began to fray, revealing the brittle threads of manipulation and control beneath.

The lies unfolded subtly, wrapped in affection and care. "You know I'd do anything for you," Liam would say with a smile, a phrase she took to mean love and devotion. But Sophie soon learned that "anything" translated to her world shrinking around her—a world where her needs and aspirations became secondary to his. Every minor disagreement was painted as a betrayal, and each assertion of independence was labeled as a lack of commitment.

Suddenly, one night, it all came crashing down around her. Liam had asked that she pick up a newspaper on the way home from work. Being tired, she forgot to grant his wishes. Before she knew what was happening, Sophie felt the sting of his fist on her lip as blood poured down her chin. But it didn't stop there. Liam grabbed her by the hair and shoved her into the wall. Losing her balance, she falls to the floor. Suddenly, he was on top of her, his hands on her throat. She must have blacked out because from there, all she remembers is waking up in the hospital.

Sensing her distress, the neighbors quickly called for help; they were concerned for her well-being. Sophie had initially hesitated about leasing an apartment, but in that moment of fear and uncertainty, she found comfort in the decision. Had they chosen to rent a house out in the country, things might have turned out tragically different, and she couldn't shake off the thought that she could have lost her life that night. It was hard to see it at the time, but perhaps God had a way of guiding her to where she needed to be. As for Liam, his arrest that night opened a door for Sophie—a chance to break free from a situation that had become unbearable.

A month later, on a breezy autumn evening in a small town, the shadows stretched long across the streets as the sun dipped below the horizon. Sophie found herself walking the familiar path to the park, her thoughts swirling like the leaves that danced around her feet. Just a few months ago, her life had felt completely different, and that night—the night everything changed—still haunted her mind.

Liam had always been a complicated person. He was charming, funny, and charismatic, but beneath that surface lay a storm of unresolved issues. Their relationship had started off like a fairy tale, filled with laughter and adventure, but over time, the cracks began to show. Liam's struggles with his childhood trauma seeped into their lives, casting shadows on the love they once shared. It was a love that started brightly but soon became a muddled mess of confusion and pain.

Sophie paused at a bench overlooking the lake. The water shimmered under the fading light, and for a moment, she allowed herself to remember the laughter they had shared and the dreams they had built together. But just as quickly, she pushed those thoughts aside. That night had served as a brutal awakening. The words exchanged, the anger unleashed, and the realization that love isn't just about passion; it's also about understanding, communication, and healing.

She closed her eyes and took a deep breath, releasing the weight of those memories. Sophie had spent weeks in introspection, realizing that while she cared deeply for Liam, she couldn't save him from his demons. Rebuilding her life was her priority now, and with each step, she felt a little stronger.

In her quest for healing, she had turned to her passion for painting. Every brushstroke helped her channel her emotions—her grief and her joy. The local gallery had even agreed to showcase her pieces next month, a testament to the progress she had made. The idea of sharing her story through art filled her with both excitement and fear, but it was a step she was ready to take.

As she sat on the bench, Sophie pulled out her journal and began to write. Words flowed like the gentle ripples on the lake. She penned down her thoughts, revealing the journey of rebuilding, learning self-love, and finding solace in her own company. For each pang of sadness, there was a note of hope. As she wrote, she envisioned the path ahead—one that was illuminated by self-discovery and new beginnings.

Sophie knew that healing was not linear and that there would be tough moments ahead. But tonight, she felt a glimmer of peace. The reminder of what love is not supposed to be had propelled her toward finding what true love means—loving oneself first, understanding boundaries, and cherishing the moments, both good and bad.

Content, she closed her journal and looked out at the lake once more. The stars began to twinkle overhead, each one a symbol of what could be—new dreams, fresh possibilities, and a life waiting to be fully embraced. And with that thought, Sophie stood up and turned towards home, ready to forge her path, one step at a time.

Expanded Learning or Group Study

In this section, you'll discover thought-provoking questions aimed at deepening your understanding of recovery from toxic relationships. Whether you're exploring these topics on your own or engaging in group discussions, these questions provide a powerful tool for personal growth and healing. Embrace the opportunity to transform your experiences and foster meaningful connections! Questions are divided into chapters.

Chapter 1

1. What are some early signs that indicate a relationship might be toxic?

2. How can gaslighting affect a person's emotional well-being over time?

3. In what ways can control manifest in a relationship without being obvious?

4. How does emotional manipulation differ from healthy communication in relationships?

5. What are the potential long-term impacts of verbal abuse on an individual's self-esteem?

6. Can you identify a situation in your life where you experienced manipulative behavior? How did it affect you?

7. What steps can someone take to break free from a toxic relationship?

8. How does the Bible guide us in distinguishing between healthy and toxic relationships?

9. Are there specific scriptures that emphasize the importance of healthy boundaries in relationships?

10. What role does self-awareness play in recognizing and addressing toxic dynamics in relationships?

Chapter 2

1. What do boundaries represent in terms of personal well-being and relationships?

2. How can failing to establish boundaries lead to feelings of resentment or burnout?

3. Can you provide an example of a situation where maintaining boundaries is necessary in a friendship?

4. In what ways does the Bible address the concept of boundaries without using the term explicitly?

5. How might setting boundaries differ in romantic relationships compared to friendships?

6. What are some practical steps a person can take to identify their personal limits?

7. Why is assertive communication important when expressing boundaries to others?

8. How can one prepare for potential resistance when setting boundaries?

9. In what ways can professionals establish boundaries to avoid burnout at work?

10. How can flexibility in boundaries facilitate intimacy while also protecting well-being?

Chapter 3

1. What are some common physical symptoms that can result from unresolved trauma?

2. How does a person's response to a traumatic event define the nature of the trauma?

3. In what ways can trauma impact an individual's ability to form and maintain close relationships?

4. What role do feelings of shame and low self-esteem play in the emotional experience of trauma survivors?

5. How can trauma manifest in romantic relationships, and what patterns might emerge as a result?

6. In what ways can unresolved trauma affect friendships and create a sense of isolation?

7. How does trauma influence parenting styles and family dynamics?

8. What are some strategies that can be employed in therapy to address the effects of trauma on relationships?

9. How can a survivor begin to recognize and break unhealthy attachment styles developed due to past trauma?

10. Why is it important to understand the physical, emotional, and relational impacts of trauma in the healing process?

Chapter 4

1. What are some key elements that characterize healthy relationships, and why is each one important?

2. How can open and honest communication help in resolving conflicts within a relationship?

3. In what ways can partners demonstrate mutual respect for each other's opinions and feelings, even when they differ?

4. Why is vulnerability considered a strength in a healthy relationship?

5. How can partners support each other's individual pursuits, such as further education or personal growth?

6. What role does trust play in maintaining a healthy relationship, and how can it be built over time?

7. How can effective communication prevent misunderstandings in situations like one partner being late for an important event?

8. In what ways can mutual support enhance the overall strength of a relationship?

9. What are some common signs of toxic patterns in relationships, and how can they be addressed?

10. How important is it to establish personal boundaries in a relationship, and how can these boundaries be respected?

Chapter 5

1. What steps can you take to cultivate a deeper relationship with God in order to discern His voice more clearly?

2. Can you identify a time in your life when you had to step outside your comfort zone to follow a calling or purpose?

3. How do you personally respond to uncertainty or challenges when trying to understand God's plan for your life?

4. In what ways can you utilize your unique gifts and talents to fulfill your life's purpose as you understand it?

5. Reflect on a biblical figure's journey that resonates with your own life experiences. What lessons can you draw from their story?

6. How can you practice active listening to ensure you're hearing God's guidance amidst life's distractions?

7. What role do trusted mentors or spiritual advisors play in your understanding of God's plan for your life?

8. How do you find hope and encouragement during difficult times when it feels like your path is unclear?

9. In what ways have past trials shaped your character and helped you grow in your faith?

10. What does it mean to you to embrace the idea that God's plan may not always align with your own desires?

Chapter 6

1. What does it mean to embrace your identity in Christ, and how can you begin that journey?

2. How can past hurts influence your perception of self-worth and capabilities?

3. What are some specific lies you've believed about yourself from toxic relationships?

4. How does Psalm 139:14 speak to your inherent worth and identity?

5. In what ways can you challenge negative self-perceptions and replace them with biblical truths?

6. Why is forgiveness essential in the process of healing and reclaiming your identity?

7. How can holding onto anger and unforgiveness affect your spiritual and emotional well-being?

8. What does self-compassion look like in your daily life, and how can you practice it?

9. How can positive affirmations based on Scripture transform your mindset?

10. What role do spiritual disciplines like prayer, meditation, and Bible study play in strengthening your identity?

11. How can being part of a faith community support your healing journey?

12. What steps can you take to surround yourself with supportive relationships that encourage your growth?

13. How can setbacks in your journey be viewed as opportunities for growth and reliance on God's grace?

14. Why is it important to celebrate small successes along your healing journey?

15. How can journaling assist in documenting your progress and processing your emotions?

This appendix provides supplementary resources to aid your healing and personal growth journey.

Appendix A: A Prayer for Healing and Release: Lord, I approach You today with a heart burdened and weary, weighed down by the painful memories of past hurts that seem to echo in my mind. I earnestly seek Your compassionate touch to heal the deep wounds I carry and restore my spirit, renewing me from the inside out. Help me to find the strength to forgive not only those who have caused me pain but also myself for holding onto this hurt for far too long.

As I step away from this toxic relationship, which has drained my energy and clouded my joy, guide me toward a healthier path filled with love and positivity. Surround me with Your divine light, illuminating my journey and helping me see the beauty and potential that lie ahead. Fill my heart with a vibrant sense of hope and joy that can overshadow the darkness I've experienced.

I long for the peace that only You can offer—a tranquility that transcends circumstances and numbs the chaos that often invades my thoughts. Please soothe my anxious mind, calming the storms of worry and fear that swirl within me. Help me to embrace the faith that You have a purposeful and beautiful plan for my life, one that holds promise and fulfillment.

Lord, I ask for Your profound healing on my emotions, mending my broken heart so I may experience joy and contentment once again. As I release the weight of resentment and bitterness, grant me the bravery to let go of the harmful ties that have kept me in a cycle of pain. Instead, help me to fully trust in Your wisdom and timing.

Finally, give me the courage to forgive those who have hurt me, allowing Your grace to wash over my feelings and replace anger with understanding. May I find peace in this release, embracing the liberation that comes from letting go. Thank you, Lord, for Your love and for walking with me on this journey toward healing. Amen.

Appendix B: Journaling Prompts for Self-Reflection: (1) Write down all the negative things about yourself that you were told during your relationship. Now, counter each one with a positive statement

(2) Write down 5 positive 'I am' affirmations about yourself and repeat them every day, e.g., "I am absolute perfection just the way I am."

(3) What was the first red flag in your relationship?

(4) What made you stay in your relationship as long as you did?

(5) What was the final straw that caused you to leave?

(6) How have you grown as a person through you relationship?

(7) What boundaries will you set with your future relationships?

(8) Are there any emotions you're avoiding?

(9) Do you require external validation?

(10) Did you ever have a gut feeling that things weren't right in your relationship? What caused you not to act upon it?

(11) When it comes to love and relationships, what is your biggest fear?

(12) After a relationship ends, it's the perfect time to reinvent yourself. Which parts of you would you like to resurrect, and which parts would you like to leave behind?

Appendix C: Boundary Setting Worksheet: There are seven types of boundaries you may need to consider. I have listed them below. In a journal or notebook, write out each boundary and detail your boundaries under each section.

(1) **Physical boundaries** protect your space and body, your right not to be touched, to have privacy, and to meet your physical needs, such as resting or eating. A physical boundary clearly defines that your body and personal space belong to you.

(2) **Sexual boundaries** protect your right to consent, to ask for what you like sexually, and to honesty about your partner's sexual history. They define what kind of sexual touch and intimacy you want, how often, when, where, and with whom.

(3) **Emotional or mental boundaries** protect your right to have your own feelings criticized or validated and not have to take care of other people's feelings. Emotional boundaries differentiate your feelings from other people, so you're accountable for your own feelings, but not responsible for how others feel. Emotional boundaries also allow us to create emotional safety by respecting each other's feelings, not oversharing personal information that's inappropriate for the nature or level of closeness in the relationship.

(4) **Spiritual boundaries** protect your right to believe in what you want, worship as you wish, and practice your spiritual or religious beliefs.

(5) **Financial and material boundaries** protect your financial resources and possessions, you right to spend your money as you choose, to not give or loan you money or possessions

if you don't want to, and your right to be paid by an employer as agreed.

(6) **Time boundaries** protect how you spend your time. They protect you from agreeing to do things you don't want to do, having people waste your time, and being overworked.

(7) **Non-negotiable boundaries** are deal-breakers, things that you absolutely must have in order to feel safe, they usually pertain to safety issues such as physical violence, emotional abuse, drug or alcohol use, fidelity, and life-threatening health issues.

This glossary defines key terms used throughout the book:

Co-dependency: An emotional and behavioral condition where a person relies too much on another person for their emotional well-being, often at the expense of their own health and independence.

Gaslighting: A form of emotional abuse where someone manipulates another person into questioning their own sanity, memory, or perception of reality.

Healthy Boundaries: Limits and expectations that protect one's physical, emotional, and spiritual well-being.

Toxic Relationship: Any relationship characterized by emotional abuse, manipulation, control, or disrespect.

Trauma: A deeply distressing or disturbing experience.

Manipulation: A form of abuse where someone tries to control you. Toxic or manipulative people may try to control your actions, decisions, or relationships with others. They may use guilt, intimidation, or threats to get their way.

Valor: Great courage in the face of danger, especially in battle.

Sources used for reference are:

Meriam- Webster online dictionary

Gateway Bible Online (Several translations used)

Acknowledgements

First and foremost, I offer my heartfelt gratitude to God, the ultimate source of strength, wisdom, and comfort. This book would not have been possible without His grace and guidance. I am deeply indebted to the many individuals who have shared their stories of overcoming toxic relationships, their vulnerability inspiring hope and resilience in others. Their courage in sharing their experiences has been instrumental in shaping this book.

I extend my sincere appreciation to Kiara Espinoza for helping with editing and for her insightful feedback, meticulous attention to detail, and unwavering support throughout the writing process. Her attention to detail and guidance were invaluable in shaping this manuscript into its final form. A special thank you to Brandie Fowler and Hannah Espinoza for their invaluable contributions of time and advice.

To my family and friends, thank you for your patience, understanding, and unwavering encouragement during the demanding process of writing this book. Your love and support have been a constant source of strength. To my husband, son, and grandbabies, thank you for understanding my absence while working. Finally, a big thank you to God—the one who gave me the ability and insight to do what I do.

Finally, to all those who have been affected by toxic relationships, I pray that this book offers comfort, hope, and a pathway to healing and restoration in Christ.

ABOUT THE AUTHOR

Karen Pless Gaines is a Christian life coach and pastor with many years of experience in counseling and biblical studies. She has a background in non-fiction writing with books like: Perfectly Imperfect Woman of God: Uniquely You, Breaking the Silence: Generational Curse Breakers, and A Warrior Heart: A Woman's Path to God. She has a passion for helping individuals overcome life's challenges through the transformative power of faith and practical strategies. Karen Pless Gaines is dedicated to guiding individuals on a path towards healing, wholeness, and a life deeply rooted in Christ.

www.ingramcontent.com/pod-product-compliance
Lightning Source LLC
Chambersburg PA
CBHW060156050426
42446CB00013B/2856